I Hear America Singing!

I Hear America Singing!

HAZEL ARNETT

GREAT FOLK SONGS FROM THE REVOLUTION TO ROCK

A Frank E. Taylor Book
Praeger Publishers · New York

MUSIC ARRANGEMENTS: Carl Miller
with Hazel Arnett

WOOD CARVINGS: Al Pisano

LINE DRAWINGS: Paul Steinberg

784.49
Ar6t

Thanks to Bess Michaels for mining library stacks . . . to
Claude Conyers for masterminding production details . . . to
folk songsmiths and music publishers for granting permission
to reproduce their properties.

Published in the United States of America in 1975
by Praeger Publishers, Inc.
111 Fourth Avenue, New York, N.Y. 10003

Library of Congress Cataloging in Publication Data
Main entry under title:

I hear America singing!

"A Frank E. Taylor book."
1. Folk-songs, American. I. Arnett, Hazel.
M1629.I17   784.4'973   74-30703

ISBN 0-275-53690-4 (cloth)
ISBN 0-275-63910-X (paperback)

Printed in the United States of America

Loving someone is asking that person to grow. As the pressures of *I Hear America Singing!* created the space, letting go simply happened, to the wonder of me and my young daughter Hayley. In celebration, I dedicate this book to her.

Contents

I Hear America Singing!

(1770s-1789)

1
BIRTH OF AMERICAN SONG
(1770s-1789)

Amidst the roar of a revolution, the young country found its voice and the people sang their own songs for the very first time. They rallied with "The Liberty Song" and "Free America," mocked with "Yankee Doodle," reported "The Battle of the Kegs" and went a-wooing with "Jenny Jenkins" and "The Young Man Who Wouldn't Hoe Corn." How fitting that the Revolution should rock the cradle of American song at a time of new beginnings and new challenges.

All too often the historical threads of a subject are nothing more than a bold design of dates and declarations—the fine shadings giving it perspective nowhere to be found. To use this style in reliving the birth of American song would be to rob it of its very breath. What follows is an overview fleshed out with life's little details.

Short tempers, strong feelings, and freedom fever were on the rise in the stormy era preceding nationhood. In the eye of the storm were Jefferson, Franklin and Washington, Adams and Hancock. There were the battles of Bunker Hill and Brandywine and the raids of John Paul Jones. Tom Paine's "Common Sense" stirred people to act, the rallying broadside came into its own, and anti-British feelings came to the boil. As more people fell into step, taking up liberty's cause, the first "Buy American" campaigns swept the colonies. The affluent renounced luxuries—silk, silver, and tea. Young ladies of good southern families vowed to spurn suitors not heeding the call. Hardy women up north formed companies of reapers and moved from farm to farm bringing in the harvest. In marathon spinning bees, the looms were never silent. Sheets and blankets were turned into makeshift uniforms and the troops wearing them nicknamed "Homespuns" by the sneering British. Not a corner of colonial life was untouched by the war. After Bunker Hill, Washington issued a call for pewter and lead.

Family treasures soon became bullets. While events surrounding the Revolution were the subjects of many songs, the lion's share sprang from the hearts and minds of a people caught up in the day-to-day struggle for survival.

As the fledgling state moved from dependence to independence and toward an egalitarian society, new strengths were summoned, new skills developed. Property, not inheritance, determined class. Mobility was both horizontal and vertical—one could move from place to place or up and down the social scale. A social climber didn't have to change professions to achieve wealth. One could work with metals as a slave or be urban gentry like silversmith Paul Revere.

It wasn't long before cities were a-bustle with artisans offering all manner of goods and services. In the clothing trade alone there were hatters, glovers, dressmakers, tailors, and shoemakers, to name a few; with shoemakers in turn using tanners, curriers, leather dressers, lastmakers, and heelmakers. Each trade had its string of specialists, be it wood, metal, glass, clay, paper, or fabric; each specialist performed tasks according to his rank as master craftsman, journeyman, or apprentice. Hours were long—twelve to sixteen a day—and business was done mostly on credit. Craftsmen were by far the largest segment of the urban population. Professional men came next—doctors, lawyers, teachers, clergymen, and sea captains; then shopkeepers, innkeepers, and the like. Townsmen spent hours over coffee framing local laws and ordinances. Small cities became the seedbed of the middle class. At the top of the pyramid were the owners of vast property and business interests; at the bottom, an almost negligible servant class.

Revolutionary America produced enough wealth to save even its poor from suffering. The greatest number lived adequately; many, comfortably; and a privileged few, in real luxury. The elite in Philadelphia, Boston, New York, Charleston, and Williamsburg enjoyed the glitter of parties, balls, assemblies; chamber concerts, masques, and other entertainments, often in luxurious settings. But ordinary Americans had to entertain themselves in the reflected glow of the hearth with songs and a bit of foottapping.

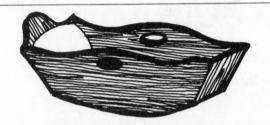

Near century's end: activity up and down and across the land. Many New Englanders moved on to Ohio; Pennsylvania settlers, to Kentucky and Tennessee. By the time George Washington was inaugurated there were ninety-two newspapers and nine colleges, among them William and Mary, Harvard, and Yale. Trade was brisk enough with the West Indies and China to support two large shipbuilding centers, one in New England, the other in Philadelphia. At home and abroad, commerce was thriving. Inland waterways were giving way to roads (once Indian footpaths) or turnpikes. Post riders carried the mail, coaches lurched in and out of ruts, and American inventiveness had produced the first steamboat, plus things as disparate as bifocal glasses and the Morgan horse. The states were united, yet divided into three distinct regions.

The life-styles of New England, the Middle Atlantic states, and the South may have developed differently, the result of climate, raw materials and ethnic composition, but the reality that survival was a family enterprise requiring long hours and hard work was shared by all. For the majority, the land was home; for the minority, the small city or town.

In New England where working the soil was hard, raising crops and tending livestock were but two of the farmer's endless tasks. The farmer-craftsman, a New England breed and progenitor of the Yankee peddler, was his own carpenter, shoemaker, tanner, toolmaker, blacksmith, and veterinarian. Home manufacture was a family way of life with the sheep and flax producing wool and linen, leather, rope, and clothes. Store-bought items were limited to gunpowder, shot, an occasional purchase of crockery or glassware and, for the table, sugar, salt, molasses, coffee, and rum. Homegrown chicory was added to coffee, and the blue wrapping paper from the sugar cone was used for dyeing cloth, in lieu of costly indigo. Be-

sides these items, no one ever thought of buying food.

Diets were simple, but hardy. There was bean porridge hot, bean porridge cold, brown bread, hominy with milk, flapjacks, pork, salt beef, fish and fowl, dairy foods, vegetables, fruit and pumpkin pudding. When wheat was in short supply, "rye and Injun" (corn and rye meals mixed) would do. Depending on how the hunting and catching ran, meat and fish might be served at every meal. Corn or buckwheat puddings came steaming to the table at noon. Root cellars were filled with cheeses, barrels of cider, corned beef and salt pork, crocks of pickles and preserves. Rafters were strung with dried fruits and vegetables. All staples so necessary to sustain the long, cold winter.

Tending the kitchen garden fell to the farmer's wife, as did feeding the chickens and collecting the eggs—the egg money hers to spend as she wished at the crossroads store. At harvest time she and the children helped in the fields, despite the never ending chores to be done around the compact frame house—an unrelenting round of cooking; cleaning; preserving; churning butter; making cheese, lard, candles, and soap; concocting medicinal syrups, salves, and ointments—for it was the farmer's wife who doctored the family, friends, and, on occasion, even the animals. In addition, linen and wool had to be carded, spun, and woven, then stitched into clothes, household linens, and sacks for grain. There was washing, ironing, bleaching and dyeing, knitting and needlework or cutting down worn clothes for the children. But it didn't end there; with the scraps that were left there were quilts to be pieced and rugs to be braided.

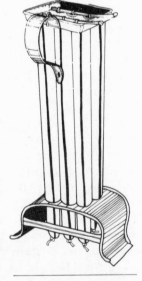

Children were rarely idle, although few went to school. They, like the adults, had chores and little time for play. But when they did, tag, blindman's bluff, leapfrog, and cat's cradle were favorites, as were singing games: "Ring Around a Rosy," "Here We Go Round the Mulberry Bush," "I Put My Right Foot In," and "London Bridge Is Falling Down." Many a boy whittled his own whistle, slingshot, or windmill, while girls made and dressed their own dolls.

Courting took place outdoors when weather was mild and by the fireside when cold. With children tucked in their trundle beds, parents soon made excuses to absent themselves. Making themselves scarce in such small houses was quite a trick.

The high point of the week was the Sabbath, when chores were few and dressing up felt good; the men in woolen jackets, linen shirts, and leather pants, the women and children in dresses of linsey-woolsey or calico, and on everyone's feet, buckled shoes. Seeing friends and neighbors was a welcome change, too. A day spent in worship, hard benches and long sermons notwithstanding, seemed to renew the spirit and reinforce courage for the arduous week ahead. On the whole, it was a hard life and a pious one punctuated with lecture days, prayers, fasting, Bible reading, and hymn singing. Compared to New Englanders, settlers in the Middle Atlantic states seemed almost jolly.

And with good reason. The climate was less harsh, the resources more varied, the soil richer, and the mix of continental blood and customs far greater. Family life was less rigid, although these settlers too were a frugal, industrious lot, working from daybreak to backache. There was the New York colony, primarily settled by the Dutch who, unlike the Huguenots in search of religious freedom, had come to trade with the Indians. They were farmers, trappers, hunters, and traders with a rugged style on the frontier and quite a comfortable one wherever regular exchanges with the mother country existed. They were an easygoing, sociable people with a fondness for food and ale. Their houses—stone, brick, or shingled—had low-pitched roofs, dutch doors, and chimneys at either end, polished floors, delft tiles, and alcove bedsteads. If more cooking utensils, linens, pewter, and silver than might be found in Yankee abodes gave hints of their more pleasurable, relaxed way of life, the ever present tankard and clay pipe confirmed it. So appealing was this style, it influenced neighboring New Jersey, which developed along similar lines with the good green earth as a base.

Of those who settled Pennsylvania, the Germans came with a fine music tradition, particularly Moravian church members, who sang hymns in four-part, even seven-part harmony—quite a contrast to the unison singing everywhere else. Religious, yet less dour than New Englanders, their lives were shaped by rules of decency that fostered strong communal ties. Schools were rare except those run by the Moravians. Children, however, were well schooled in crafts. Both sexes knitted; the girls, stockings; the boys, suspenders.

Aside from farming, the terrain was rich with ore and conducive to many trades learned in the old country—giving rise to grist mills, lumber mills, and paper mills, glassworks, and crockery works. Gunsmiths and ironmasters produced the first cast-iron cook stove, the Pennsylvania rifle, and the Conestoga wagon, forerunner of the "prairie schooner."

The tall, stone houses of Pennsylvania were roofed in tile and painted with flowers, hex symbols, or both, as were barns, benches, and chests. Out of their kitchens came cornmeal mush, apple butter, sauerkraut, and a variety of pies, main dish and dessert. And out back they dug pits, lined them with ice cut from rivers and ponds, stored all manner of foods for months. Life may not have been easy, but they wanted for little.

The frontier during revolutionary times stretched the length of the Alleghenies. The pioneers who faced its ceaseless dangers sprang from rugged Scotch-Irish stock. In a land where conflict with Indians was constant, men built sturdy cabins, blockhouses, and forts.

They hunted, fished, trapped, cleared the land, and planted grain. Their women pounded the corn, cooked the catch, collected the eggs, milked the cow, and, to tide them over lean times, smoked, salted, powdered, and dried all available food.

Men's garments, leggings and moccasins included, were fashioned of deerskin with a layer of linsey next to the skin; caps and jackets, of native fur. A bullet bag, tomahawk, and scalping knife hung from a thick leather belt; rifles were carried in hand. Women wore pretty much what they'd brought with them, replacing worn fabrics with deerskin. When shoes gave out, people almost always went barefoot.

The wilderness also furnished and fed. Buffalo and bear skins became beds, timber split into flat slabs made tables and benches or, scooped out like a rolling trough, cradles. Yet utensils and vessels crudely wrought from wood held the richest milk and butter, the choicest game—not infrequently, buffalo tongue. Visitors were rare, but occasionally an adventurous peddler found his way to the door. To isolated settlers he was company, usually welcome. His goods were needed; his news or tattle (often in ballad form), a source of entertainment.

The South, once called the four kingdoms—of tobacco, cotton, rice, and sugar—was essentially aristocratic, slave-owning, and agricultural, with huge, isolated plantations drawing wealth from the land. The slave system produced few craftsmen, outside those trained by transient artisans to fulfill basic needs. Trade with England had kept the artisan class from developing and when the Revolution cut off that trade, its lack was sorely felt.

Compact as was the New England house, the southern one was diffuse. Behind the main house of lime-covered brick with columns and multipaned windows, a series of detached buildings: smokehouses, cold spring houses (their coolers), kitchens, laundries, workshops, tool shacks, and slave quarters. This arrangement not only kept the master separate, but his house cool. The master ran the plantation, but his lady managed the huge staff of black "house slaves" and white, college-bred tutors and masters of music and dance. Contrary to her flighty image, she was very capable. She had to be to keep the machinery running. She was mistress, manager, doctor, nurse, counsellor, seamstress, housekeeper, and mother all rolled into one. Keeper of the keys and recipes, she set a fine table, often with great meals rivaling a restaurant menu: oysters, beaten biscuits, and hominy; saddle of fine mutton, baked ham, fried chicken, beef, turkey, and duck; assorted vegetables—sweet potatoes, of course; for dessert, plum pudding, pies, tarts, and ice cream; and to drink, madeira, port, and bourbon. But poor folks, slaves particularly, ate what's called soul food today—pig's knuckles, chitlins, grits, and greens—and drank crude corn liquor.

Plantation style wasn't the only life-style in the South of those days. Immigrant colonists also utilized the natural riches of wood, field, and stream. They felled the trees, put up the log cabins, worked the land, and quickly joined the ranks of independent farmers—the backbone of revolutionary society.

The foundation of American national song is firmly rooted in the British tradition. This came about rather naturally since the greatest number of seventeenth- and eighteenth-century immigrants were English-speaking. Therefore, the first songs sung in the new country were traditional songs brought from the old country. Providing a common tradition, a common literature, and a common morality, they were most effective as a unifying force in a harsh, new world.

Before very long a number of traditional songs underwent Americanization, as new lyrics were put to old tunes—a process still going on today. Eventually, wholly American songs appeared with both new words and new music.

Early settlers had sung, still sang, the traditional songs from memory, passing them on by word of mouth. Most of the new ballads were written down, with the printing press playing an important role in their dissemination. They were sung, for the most part, without accompaniment; not because people didn't want to use instruments, but because conditions rarely permitted such luxury. Playing a fiddle is well nigh impossible when plowing, cooking, nursing a baby, or felling a tree.

Although most singing was unaccompanied, the settlers did have instruments. Aboard ship there was apt to be a jaw's harp or a fiddle. Black slaves developed the fretless banjo. The Scots brought bagpipes to North Carolina as well as to New York. Country folk created a variety of instruments, among them the plucked dulcimer found in the mountains of Kentucky and Tennessee. And finally, the fife and drum, which everybody knows accompanied colonials as they marched off to war.

Singing, then as now, provided a buffer against loneliness or gave a sense of community in a group. Social events in the olden days, usually part of the work picture, knit communities together: quilting

bees and singing parties in the winter, barn and house "raisings" in the spring and summer, husking and chopping bees in the fall.

There were songs for everybody and everything. Probably the most moving ones were the broadside ballads that came out of the war itself. They gave the news in verse form, complete with editorial comment, and were, in effect, singing newspapers. They reported battles, celebrated triumphs, kidded the enemy, boosted morale, and extolled heroes. What better way then, to get in touch with one's own roots and traditions in the American Revolution, than to sing these songs—the songs of the people who made these United States possible!

Old Colony Times

Traditional

Cheerfully

1. In good old col-o-ny times, When we were un-der the king
2. The first he was a Miller, And the second he was a Weaver,

Three rogu-ish chaps fell in-to mis-haps, Be-cause they could not sing.
And the third he was a lit-tle Tai - lor, Three rogu-ish chaps to-gether.

REFRAIN

Be - cause they could not sing, Be-cause they could not sing; Three_

rogu-ish chaps fell in-to mis-haps Be-cause they could not sing.

3. Now the Miller he stole corn,
   And the Weaver he stole yarn,
   And the little Tailor stole broadcloth for
   To keep these three rogues warm. [Refrain]

4. The Miller got drown'd in his dam,
   The Weaver got hung in his yarn,
   And the devil clapp'd his claw on the little Tailor,
   With the broadcloth under his arm. [Refrain]

Revolutionary Tea

Traditional

3. And so the old lady her servant called up
   And packed off a budget of tea;
   And eager for three pence a pound,
   She put in enough for a large familie.
   She order'd her servants to bring home the tax,
   Declaring her child should obey,
   Or old as she was, and almost woman grown,
   She'd half whip her life away.

4. The tea was conveyed to the daughter's door,
   All down by the ocean's side;
   And the bouncing girl pour'd out every pound
   In the dark and boiling tide;
   And then she called out to the Island Queen,
   "O mother, dear mother," quoth she,
   "Your tea you may have when 'tis steep'd enough
   But never a tax from me."

The Young Man Who Wouldn't Hoe Corn

Traditional

3. He went to the fence and there peeped in,
   The weeds and the grass came up to his chin;
   The weeds and the grass they grew so high,
   They caused this young man for to sigh.

4. So he went down to his neighbor's door,
   Where he had often been before:
   "Pretty little miss, will you marry me?
   Pretty little miss, what do you say?"

5. "Here you are, a-wanting for to wed
   And cannot make your own cornbread!"
   "Single I am, single I'll remain,
   A lazy man I'll not maintain."

Jenny Jenkins

With spirit

Traditional

mf 1. Will you wear white, my __ dear, O my dear? Will you wear white, Jen-ny
2. Will you wear green, my __ dear, O my dear? Will you wear green, Jen-ny

Jen - kins? No, I won't wear white, It is much too bright.
Jen - kins? No, I won't wear green, 'Cause it can't be seen.

REFRAIN

I will buy me a fol - di - rol - di - till - di - toll - di Seek a dou - ble
cresc.

Use - a - cause - a - roll - a - find - a - me - a - roll, _____ Jen-ny Jen-kins, roll.
al fine

3. "Will you wear brown, my dear, O my dear?
Will you wear brown, Jenny Jenkins?"
"No, I won't wear brown,
As it makes me frown." [*Refrain*]

4. "Will you wear red, my dear, O my dear?
Will you wear red, Jenny Jenkins?"
"No, I won't wear red,
Since it goes to my head." [*Refrain*]

5. "Will you wear blue, my dear, O my dear?
Will you wear blue, Jenny Jenkins?"
"No, I won't wear blue,
For I don't love you." [*Refrain*]

[11]

The Spinning Wheel

Traditional

Free America

Music: Traditional
Words by *Joseph Warren*

Con spirito

1. That seat of sci - ence, A - thens, And earth's proud mis - tress,
2. We led fair Frank - lin hith - er, And, lo! the des - ert

Rome. Where now are all their glo - ries? We
smiled; A par - a - dise of pleas - ure Was

scarce can find a tomb. Then guard your rights, A -
o - pened to the world. Your har - vest, bold A -

mer - i - cans, Nor stoop to law - less sway, ____ Op -
mer - i - cans, No pow'r shall snatch a - way, ____ Huz -

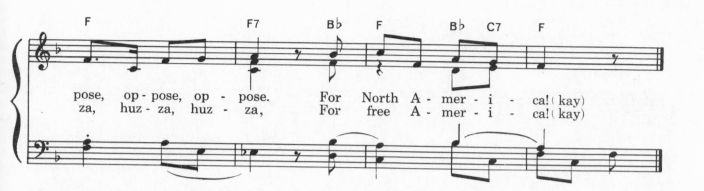

pose,   op - pose, op - pose.   For   North   A - mer - i - ca!(kay)
za,   huz - za,   huz - za,   For   free   A - mer - i - ca!(kay)

3. Torn from a world of tyrants,
    Beneath this western sky,
    We formed a new dominion,
    A land of liberty.
    The world shall own we're masters here;
    Then hasten on the day:
    Huzza, huzza, huzza,
    For free America.

4. God bless this maiden climate,
    And through its vast domain
    May hosts of heroes cluster,
    Who scorn to wear a chain;
    And blast the venal sycophant
    That dares our rights betray;
    Huzza, huzza, huzza,
    For free America.

5. Lift up your heads, ye heroes,
    And swear with proud disdain
    The wretch that would ensnare you
    Shall lay his snares in vain;
    Should Europe empty all her force,
    We'll meet her in array,
    And fight, and shout, and fight and shout
    For free America.

6. Some future day shall crown us
    The masters of the main.
    Our fleets shall speak in thunder
    To England, France, and Spain;
    And the nations o'er the ocean's spread
    Shall tremble and obey
    The sons, the sons, the sons,
    Of brave America.

Smithfield Mountain

3. Scarce had he mowed across the fiel'
   When a pizen sarpint bit his heel-eel-eel-eel-eel.
   Riturilurila.

4. "O, Maury Ann, oh don't you see?
   A great big sarpint done bit me-me-me-me-me."
   Riturilurila.

Tom, Tom, the Piper's Son

Yankee Doodle

Traditional

Bright march

1. Fa - ther and I went down to camp, A - long with Cap - tain
2. And there we see a swamp-ing gun, Large as a log of

Good - ing, And there we see the men and boys As
ma - ple. Up - on a deuc - ed lit - tle cart A

REFRAIN

thick as has - ty pud - ding. Yan - kee doo - dle keep it up,
load for fa - ther's cat - tle.

Yan - kee doo - dle dan - dy, Mind the mu - sic
'Neath the fig tree

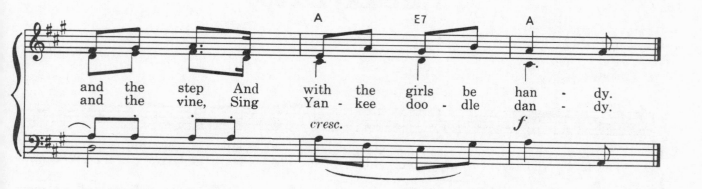

and the step And with the girls be han - dy.
and the vine, Sing Yan - kee doo - dle dan - dy.

cresc.　　　　　　　　*f*

3. And every time they shoot it off,
   It takes a horn of powder,
   It makes a noise like father's gun,
   Except a nation louder. [*Refrain*]

4. Cousin Simon grew so bold,
   I thought he would have cocked it,
   It scared me so I streaked it off,
   And hung to father's pocket. [*Refrain*]

5. And there I see a pumpkin shell
   As big as mother's basin,
   And every time they touched it off,
   I scampered like the nation. [*Refrain*]

6. Nor stopped, as I remember,
   It scared me so I scampered off,
   Nor turn'd about till I got home,
   Locked up in mother's chamber. [*Refrain*]

7. I see a little barrel, too,
   The heads were made of leather;
   They knock'd upon't with little clubs,
   And called the folks together. [*Refrain*]

8. And there was Captain Washington,
   And gentle folks about him;
   They say he's grown so 'tarnal proud,
   He will not ride without 'em. [*Refrain*]

9. He got him on his meeting clothes,
   Upon a slapping stallion,
   He set the world along in rows,
   In hundreds and in millions. [*Refrain*]

10. Yankee Doodle went to town
    A-riding on a pony,
    Stuck a feather in his cap
    And called it macaroni. [*Refrain*]

The Lucky Escape

Traditional

Wistfully

1. I that once was a plough - man, a sail - or am now. No
2. I did not much like for to be a - board a ship, When in

lark that a - loft in the sky Ev - er
dan - ger there is no door to creep out. I

flut - ter'd his wings to give speed to the plough Was so
liked the jol - ly tars, I liked bum - bo and flip, But I

gay and so care - less as I, Was so gay and so care - less as
did not like rock - ing a - bout, But I did not like rock - ing a -

3. At last safe I landed, and in a whole skin,
   Nor did I make any long stay,
   Ere I found by a friend who I ax'd for my kin,
   Father dead, and my wife run away!
   "Ah, who but thyself," said I, "has thou to blame?
   Wives loosing their husbands oft lose their good name.
       Ah, why did I roam
       When so happy at home;
       I could sow and could reap,
   Ere I left my poor plough to go ploughing the deep.
       When so sweetly the horn
       Call'd me up in the morn,
   Curse light upon the Carsindo and the inconstant wind,
   That made me for to go and leave my dear behind."

4. "Why if that be the case," said this very same friend,
   "And you ben't no more minded to roam,
   Gi'e's a shake by the fist, all your care's at an end,
   Dad's alive and your wife's safe at home."
   Stark staring with joy, I leapt out of my skin,
   Buss'd my wife, mother, sister, and all of my kin.
       "Now," cried I, "let them roam,
       Who want a good home,
       I am well, so I'll keep;
   Nor again leave my plough to go ploughing the deep.
       Once more shall the horn
       Call me up in the morn,
   Nor shall any damn'd Carsindo, nor the inconstant win
   Ere tempt me for to go and leave my dear behind."

(1790-1815)

2

ONE NATION, LAND OF LIBERTY
(1790-1815)

The fledgling republic, far from settling down, charged forward. The Bill of Rights, the court system, cabinet posts, and administrative departments would come out of the fiery first Congress. The economy would spurt ahead with a rush of trade as budding industry changed the face of the North and Whitney's cotton gin the fate of the South. It was a time that found people on the move—some settling in towns, others opening frontiers far beyond the Appalachians. But wherever they lived and whatever their lot, Americans believed in life, liberty, and the pursuit of happiness. With Jefferson, the Louisiana Purchase, and the War of 1812, the country's rhythm soon quickened. And never missing a beat, folk songs faithfully mirrored the times: a visionary election campaign in "Jefferson and Liberty," the pioneer's plaintive cry in "Wayfaring Stranger," the boasts of "The Hunters of Kentucky" how they beat the British at New Orleans.

The tide of the Revolution had receded, but crosscurrents of controversy still swirled around the ship of state, with Hamilton and Jefferson on the forecastle and Washington at the helm. The struggle was on between the monied and the masses, and Tom Paine's *Rights of Man* riled the political waters. Those interpreting the Constitution literally would come to believe in centralized power; those defining it loosely, in states' rights. Out of the political contest between Federalist and Republican, the two-party system would come to be, a concept never dreamed of by the nation's builders.

The new government had to take several preliminary steps before the constitutional blueprint became a functioning machine. Fortunately, it could call on some distinguished leaders: Washington, Hamilton, Jefferson and Webster, John Marshall, Patrick Henry, and a few others. Within little more than a decade the number of agencies, and the machinery for others, set up by Congress, was quite impressive: the authorization of the mint; the Naturalization Act, anticipating mass immigration; the outlawing of African slave trade, despite its squeeze on the cotton kingdom; the Copyright Act and the opening of the patent office. In an attempt to raise revenue, Hamilton put an excise tax on whiskey. Pennsylvania farmers staged the Whiskey Rebellion. Washington's army quelled it and proved the new government's strength in domestic relations. At the same time, the country was forced to prove itself in foreign relations as the Reign of Terror following the French Revolution pressed hard on its business nerve. It was decided that partiality toward Britain or France would be disastrous, that the states desperately needed a breather to grow. For a while then, neutrality was the answer. It would be 1812 before war was declared on Britain, at which time the first U.S. war bonds were issued. Although Washington had paved the way for the basically isolationist policy of the nineteenth century, the United States took on the role of world benefactor rather early in its history when Congress responded to a Venezuelan earthquake with the First Foreign Aid Act.

As over five million Americans confidently moved into the nineteenth century with a new president (Jefferson) and a new capital (Washington), the country was sufficiently bountiful for a foreign visitor to observe that nowhere in the world was food so abundant and varied. Largely responsible for this were the farmers who, in their quest for richer land, had rolled back frontier upon frontier. If farming methods had not changed much, thinking among gentlemen farmers had. They believed farming could be improved by scientific methods. Many established agricultural societies, and all encouraged research. There were studies on how to improve crop yields and harvesting methods, how to popularize rotation and fertilizers, with county fairs and farm journals set up to publicize their findings. Yet the impact on the average dirt farmer was negligible. The fear of trying something new doomed Charles Newbold's iron plow to failure. Most farmers claimed it would poison the soil.

There were many Newbolds whose visions and imagination pointed the nation in the direction of future greatness. The first generation of engineers, surveyors, scientists, and inventors emerged, and their plans, drawings, and dreams passed through the newly opened patent office. Eli Whitney invented the cotton gin and became father of U.S. mass production with his concept of interchangeable parts. John Fitch launched the steamboat era with his duckfeet paddlers and Robert Fulton established it with the *Clermont*'s historic run from New York to Albany and back in just five days. Other inventions: Jacob Perkins's nail-making machine; Oliver Evans's high-pressure steam engine and automated milling processes; Samuel Slater's cotton mill, where for the first time all the steps of production were under one roof; and, not too many years after that, Francis Cabot Lowell's factory in Waltham, Massachusetts, the world's first to convert raw cotton into cloth using water-powered machinery. Once the brawn had been taken out of factory work, the way was open for cheap labor. Women and children would fast become an important part of the work force. In good time textiles flowed from Rhode Island and Massachusetts; leather goods —shoes and gloves—from neighboring New York; clocks, cutlery, and woolen hats from Connecticut; and from mining areas in Pennsylvania and Virginia all manner of things produced by the iron trade. And

if the industrial giant was in its infancy, the age of the peddler was in its prime. Besides goods, peddlers sold services. Their itinerant ranks wandered the gamut from tinkers, tailors, woodworkers, and weavers to teachers, preachers, doctors, and dentists, to printers, portrait painters, and on and on. Many served as trained observers advising would-be pioneers about areas where the soil was rich, the people prosperous, and the best routes to get there. Foot travel of the

previous period now gave way to horses, wagons, and rafts; with rafts opening the way for the general store when the more adventurous pioneer would buy "a whole raft of goods" and set up shop in the front room of his cabin. In time rafts became flatboats with enormous cabins housing whole families as they floated hundreds of miles down rivers with horses, cows, carts, plows—all their worldly belongings. As traffic on inland waterways became more popular, mules walking towpaths on banks pulled canal boats at the rate of one and a half miles per hour. A little later steam ferries designed for short distances went three miles an hour, and the large steamboats that followed were still faster. But the confinement of steamboats to lakes, rivers, and protected bays of the eastern seaboard limited their usefulness in that they failed to connect Atlantic ports with the interior. Eventually those links would be made by railroads—but that's getting ahead of the story.

So just as poor roads had forced the development of inland waterways, their very limitations dramatized the need for better highways. Before the new century came round, the first macadam road (running some sixty-two miles) and the first important turnpike opened between Philadelphia and Lancaster, Pennsylvania. Along with roads grew a need for bridges—the first wooden truss bridge built by a Colonel Hale in Vermont. With unprotected wooden spans so prone to decay, the covered bridge was to become a familiar sight in northern valleys, as were the stagecoaches traveling across them. Just as better conditions had stimulated the stagecoach business, it in turn accomplished that for the wayside inn. By the early eighteen hundreds peddlers and travelers by the thousands would be lodged for something like 30¢ a night in taverns all across New England, the Middle Atlantic states, and the South. What they lacked in cleanliness was more than made up in liveliness. The taproom served all the hard liquors known today—5¢ a glass for stagecoach riders, 3¢ for wagoners—and something called black strap or American flip, a mixture of strong beer and rum burned bitter by a white-hot poker. For entertainment there were dancing bears and jugglers in the stable yard or card playing and newspaper reading around the hearth. Food was plentiful, if a bit on the crude side, and sleeping conditions quite rugged—often no less than eleven beds to a room, five or more to a bed (no boots allowed). A wagoner's bill for bed, two meals, and feed for six horses could amount to as much as $1.75.

There was also an upsurge in travel for religious reasons, as the nation went through its second great awakening, with camp meetings attracting people like magnets. As early evangelist James McGready and, later, Peter Cartwright (credited with twelve thousand baptisms) drew huge crowds in the back country and word of their magical powers spread, great waves of revivalism rolled through Georgia, the Carolinas, Pennsylvania, Tennessee, Ohio, and Indiana. By 1811 some four hundred camp meetings, mostly in the West and South, had taken place. A typical one with nonstop praying, preaching, and singing would begin on a Thursday and not end before the following Tuesday. Wagons would arrive piled high with food and bedding; makeshift tents would be set up in fields, and bonfires tended straight through the night. The emotional element of evangelism was powerfully appealing to a frontier society of crude, scattered, lonely people where whiskey sold for 25¢ a gallon, eye-gouging fights were common, gambling was endemic, and illiteracy high. Baptist conferences meted out stiff disciplines to members caught fighting, gossiping, committing adultery, stealing or racing horses. The Baptists and the Methodists soon became

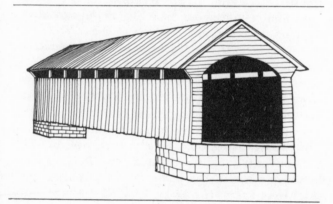

the most vital moral force in the West and most powerful sects in America. Their easily understood doctrines and informal approach—lay preachers and circuit riders—so suited pioneer life, their churches quite naturally became the social and intellectual focus of the frontier.

In rural communities located in what would later be dubbed the Bible Belt, *the* book was the single most important intellectual tool. A Parson Weems who preached on village greens and fiddled for dances and weddings was reputed to have sold three thousand. He also was the author of "The Drunkard's Looking Glass," which he sold in bars for 25¢ a copy. John Chapman, another purveyor of religious tracts, and famed for scattering apple seeds all up and down the Ohio Valley, would one day become the folk hero Johnny Appleseed.

While itinerants in the back woods hawked alma-

nacs, chapbooks, and broadsides, reading matter in most country towns was the daily newspaper, delivered to subscribers for a penny or two. Yet in Salisbury, Connecticut, the first tax-supported library opened. In large cities, the first stirrings of literary nationalism would be felt as periodicals and literary clubs encouraged native talent. Native artists Washington Irving and James Fenimore Cooper would be published and become the literary giants of the period. This was also the moment when Noah Webster's *Compendious Dictionary of the English Language* appeared, the culmination of readers, spellers, and grammars—educational materials developed by him over decades—and popular all over America.

Educators such as Webster worked to develop a distinctly American educational system. An increase in secular institutions would pit church schools against state schools in a struggle to control higher education, and the number of colleges grew from nine to thirty-seven in a mere twenty-odd years. Teachers, still held in low esteem, were paid accordingly, as little as 67¢ a week. Women continued to be shortchanged; close to 70 percent of them were illiterate. The wealthy, as before, tutored their daughters in English, French, and music, while the middle class, sniffing the winds of feminism, demanded equal education for their girls. As such early educators as Emma Willard opened female academies in their own homes, established private schools began to admit girls, giving them separate instruction in a less demanding curriculum. What started as a gesture soon became a need as men moved into factories and women filled the vacuum by moving into teaching.

Fittingly, women discarded whalebones and petticoats, and body-clinging materials would lead to warnings about morals and health. Poke bonnets would cover close-cropped hair, once piled high, and high heels give way to sandals. It would be the first time children's clothes assumed a style of their own and the first time in decades men's garb changed from head to toe. Bicornes and stovepipes would come, tricornes go, powdered hair turn natural, and knee britches grow to pantaloon length, with a patent for galluses signaling the change. Swords would disappear into canes, and cloth-topped boots called gaiters appear as footwear scaled down. The fit of shoes would be changed forever by William Young, a Philadelphia shoemaker, who made them for left and right feet instead of the same for both. So great was the demand for shoes that the small town of Lynn, Massachusetts, produced more than three hundred thousand pairs per year before 1800. By 1815 the country would be at the threshold of an industrial revolution.

America was two times its original size in area and population; five times enriched by Vermont, Kentucky, Tennessee, Ohio, and Louisiana; and three times saddened by the deaths of Franklin, Washington, and Hamilton. The Mississippi Valley was emptied of Indians and filled up with immigrants, the economy soundly based at home and competitively launched abroad. It had taken the United States just two and a half decades to move from sectionalism to nationalism, from fierce regional loyalties to fervent national pride.

Despite dissipated loyalties, however, each section developed in its own distinctive way. By 1800 New England was rich, with its politics and society controlled by sea traders, bankers, and merchants of wealth. Cultural life was dominated by the town meeting, which gave it that special Yankee flavor, and the Congregationalists. In Boston, Lyman Beecher, Harriet Stowe's father, conducted one continuous revival from the pulpit of his Hanover Street church. Attached houses by Charles Bullfinch, America's first architect, would set the city's architectural style— Boston "Federal." East Coast cities—with their many shops, banks, importers, ship suppliers, and wharves —virtually throbbed with activity.

Rural life with few exceptions continued to be heavy on chores and light on diversions. The farmer's wife was still busy round the clock: indoors, all the domestic arts and crafts; outdoors, sugaring, tending the chickens, the kitchen garden. But many of her husband's chores were now done by the local sawmill, flour mill, or itinerant craftsman, provided he turned his small surplus of grain, meat, and wood into cash. "Laziness is the worst form of original sin" the children were taught, but few had much chance to find out; their days were duty-filled. There would be paying jobs, too: caring for silkworms, the splitting of shoe pegs and, best paid, the making of birch splinter brooms (6¢ the piece). Then there was gathering: the gathering of the medicinal ginseng root for the lucrative China trade, the gathering of nuts, choke cherries for cherry rum or cherry bounce, and pounds of mulberry leaves—the task made a game with the singing of "Here We Go Round the Mulberry Bush."

Singing games filled many happy moments after chores for the very young. Everyone enjoyed ice skating when the ponds froze. For the boys, there was football with an inflated pig bladder. As for the elders, there was the merriment that went along with bees, barn raisings, and husking parties, sleigh rides, singing school, and square dancing; each occasion made merrier as the rum jug went round and the cod, corn, and apple pie went down.

Even if life-styles in New England had become less rigid, they were still far tighter than those of the Middle Atlantic states where society was more varied, less restrained, quite cosmopolitan; freer to develop diverse styles. Changes in field and forest were minimal, small towns less isolated as wheeled traffic increased and factories dotted the hillsides. But dramatic changes took place as the teeming, steaming, faster beat of two cosmopolitan centers radiated energy and excitement. The cities of New York and Philadelphia were to dominate regional society in states that would leap forward commercially and industrially. Early in the eighteen´ hundreds New York State outdistanced New England in agriculture, shipping, banking, and trade, and New York City experienced such rapid population and commercial growth it would become the nation's first city. Wall Street rivaled Philadelphia in banking and trade. More than a mile of warehouses along New York's East River presaged its future, as did the swelling stream of immigrants pouring into the Lower East Side where cobblestone streets were overrun with chickens, cattle, and the city's famous "foraging pigs." In a town where Dutch influence still prevailed, inequities were sharp. If merchants worked seven hours, factory hands worked twice that. In an atmosphere of seeming plenty where markets vended sixty-three kinds of fish and fifty-two varieties of meat and fowl (whole pigs went for 50¢), burghers ate ten-course dinners with their new four-tined forks while laborers, if lucky, would eat two-dish ones with their hands. While society might be dancing the "Tammany quick-step," attending concerts, plays, or operas in which obscenities and garbage throwing were part of the show, average New Yorkers would have to make do with a rough turn and a lusty song at the local tavern.

But culturally, New York trailed America's most elegant city, Philadelphia, center for medical and scientific study and intellectual capital of the nation. It had the most bookshops and publishing houses, the most banks and largest public market, a street system, street cleaning and watering services, excellent street lamps, a watch and patrol corps. Efficiency aside, Philadelphia had the frivolous air of a French city, even boasting a cabaret. The papers of the day were filled with advertisements for French dancing schools, dancing masters, cosmetics, pastries, and brandy.

In marked contrast, Washington, to which Jefferson had moved his administration, was a raw, half-finished city in a fever-ridden swamp. The single wing of the capitol faced seven or eight boarding houses and a mile away the president's house was surrounded by a cluster of shops and residences.

But south of the Potomac, Charleston and New Orleans surpassed Philadelphia and New York in glitter and show of easy living, even though Charleston locked its doors and blinds at ten and frowned on giddy gaiety more than Boston. Both cities, redolent of the Mediterranean with homes in ice-cream pastels, graceful verandas, lacy ironwork, fragrant gardens of semitropical plants and flowers, would enrich the country culturally and economically. Charleston, center of West Indies trade and by 1801 a port through which twenty million pounds of cotton passed annually, was to be home to America's first secular music organization, the St. Cecilia Society. New Orleans had its opera house (first in the United States), Creole folk songs and cuisine, and miles of levees overloaded with goods from near and far, the plantations and the upper Ohio Valley. As for the rural South, it took a feudal stance once cotton was crowned king. Class lines heretofore loosely drawn were now sharply defined. At the top, the great planter controlled every aspect of southern life and 75 percent of the wealth. The small planter came next, then the yeoman farmer, 75 percent of the population, who worked his own poor farm. Below him were the poor white, Georgia cracker, mountain white, and plantation black. How ironic that those at the bottom, with so little to give, should give so much. The slave of this period enriched American culture with his many spirituals and two dances in particular, the buck dance and the pigeon wing, later the buck

and wing of minstrel shows. The mountain white made a very different contribution. He preserved not only old English speech, but numberless Old World songs and ballads, such as "Barbara Allen," "Lord Randall," and "Frog Went A-Courtin'." He managed this by standing still, for he was the "stranded frontiersman" who remained isolated in a pocket of the Appalachians while the westward movement passed around him.

If some saw the West as an enchanted land of rumor and legend where bushes dripped honey, Indians spoke Welsh, and trees died from growing too fast, the majority saw it as a challenge to start anew. Lewis and Clark may have inspired some, business recessions or crowded cities pressured others, but for all, the lure was land—and it was cheap: eighty acres, ten bits apiece. Braving the hazards of getting there was a small price indeed. Many would have the courage but few the fortitude to deal with the elements, the Indians, the animals and illness, death and starvation. From the seaboard south where tobacco had worn out the soil, the lush bottom lands of the West attracted farmers who raised cotton and wheat. Back-country folk, weary of old conflicts between country and coastal areas in New York, Pennsylvania, and the Carolinas pressed on in search of personal independence as well as land. The entire country seemed to be "breaking up and moving westward" along the Hudson and Mohawk valleys, the Cumberland Gap, and wilderness roads. It was a two-pronged invasion that would end up as the Northwest and the Southwest. The soil, climate, and forest of the Northwest was fertile ground for small-scale farming, grain, and cattle. The mountainous eastern counties of the Southwest would also have its small farms, with slave-holding planters settling in the western flatlands and busy trade towns springing up along the rivers. Before too many years had elapsed three major industries would dominate the region: whiskey, meatpacking, and lumber. Only austerity in the colonial tradition —men building log cabins in less than five days, women cooking over open fires, everybody craving bread—could have accomplished so much so soon.

Daily life, for the most part, resembled that of early New England where leisure was unknown. Were it not for corn, even a semblance of social life would have been nil. But there was something about shucking, shelling, and grinding that always brought forth a rousing good folk song and a rollicking good square dance at the fiddler's call. In communities that considered the violin the devil's instrument, of course there was none of this. But as the less puritanical rolled west, cheap fiddles selling for under ten dollars were

sure to be part of the clutter and clatter of pots, pans, and possessions. At that price, no wonder the legend grew up that fiddles came in handy for frightening off wolves! Although the twang of an occasional jaw's harp might be heard on the trail, established settlers were good customers for organ peddlers, as instruments made homes social centers for miles around. But more precious than musical instruments were the songs they brought with them—many the very ones that had traveled from Old World to New. Newer songs, the white spirituals, came out of camp meetings as revival fever spread, songs set to traditional tunes with passionate messages about sin and salvation,

hellfire and brimstone. These songs were sung in the South as well and had their black counterparts in those sung by slaves attempting to blunt the agony of an oppressive destiny. Southern ladies and gentlemen sang and played the music of Europe—sacred and secular songs, baroque choral compositions, solo and chamber works for strings and woodwinds.

In the North were the glimmerings of a musical awakening, as New England shed enough puritanism to allow secular music. America's first composers, William Billings and Francis Hopkinson, were heard, America's first operas performed in New York City, America's first orchestral society established in Boston. The period saw the start of music publishing, more instrument making, more music schools, itinerant teachers, peddlers and the emergence of band music, with concerts turning into balls. An old English drinking song with new words by a Baltimore lawyer would become the national anthem. It was a time when popular songs overflowed with patriotism and politics. And a time when such songs as "Hail Columbia" and "The Hunters of Kentucky" became national airs as they were fed into the mainstream of American folk song.

Cumberland Gap

Traditional

Sassy and snappy

Wayfaring Stranger

Traditional

3. I'll soon be freed from every trial,
    My body sleep in the churchyard,
   I'll drop the cross of self-denial,
    And enter on my great reward.
   I'm going there to see my brothers
    Who've gone before me one by one,
   I'm only going over Jordan,
    I'm only going over home.

4. I want to wear a crown of glory,
    When I get home to that good land,
   I want to shout salvation's story,
    In concert with the blood-washed band.
   I'm going there to see my Saviour,
    To sing His praise forever more,
   I'm only going over Jordan,
    I'm only going over home.

A Blessing on Brandy and Beer

Rollicking along

Traditional

1. When one's drunk, not a girl but looks pret - ty, The
2. Oh, give me but plen - ty of li - quor, I'd

coun - try's as gay as the ci - ty,___ And all that one says is so
laugh at the squire and the vic - ar ___ And if I'd a wife, why I'd

wit - ty. A bless - ing on bran - dy and beer.___
kick her, If e'er she pre - tend - ed to sneer.___

REFRAIN

Bring the cup! Fill it up! Take a sup! Take a sup! And

let not the flinch-er come near, And let not the flinch-er come near.___

3. Though I know it's a heavy disaster,
   Yet I mind not the rage of my master.
   He bullies, and I drink the faster!
   A blessing on brandy and beer. [Refrain]

4. With a cherry-cheek'd maid I've an eye on,
   I do many things they cry fie on.
   Egod, I'm as bold as a lion!
   A blessing on brandy and beer. [Refrain]

The Hunters of Kentucky

Traditional

REFRAIN

O Ken- tuck - y, the hun - ters of Ken - tuck - y.

O Ken - tuck - y, the hun - ters of Ken - tuck - y.

3. I s'pose you've read it in the prints how Packenham attempted
To make Old Hick'ry Jackson wince, but soon his schemes repented;
For we with rifles ready cock'd through such occasion lucky,
And soon around the hero flock'd the hunters of Kentucky. [*Refrain*]

4. You've heard I s'pose how New Orleans is fam'd for wealth and beauty,
There's girls of ev'ry hue it seems, from snowy white to sooty;
So Packenham he made his brags, if he in fight was lucky,
He'd have their girls and cotton bags, in spite of old Kentucky. [*Refrain*]

5. A bank was raise to hide our breast, not that we thought of dying,
But that we always like to rest, unless the game is flying;
Behind it stood our little force—none wish'd it to be greater,
For ev'ry man was half a horse and half an alligator. [*Refrain*]

6. They found at last 'twas vain to fight, where lead was all their booty,
And so they wisely took a flight and left us all our beauty;
And now if danger e'er annoys, remember what our trade is;
Just send for us Kentucky boys, and we'll protect you, ladies. [*Refrain*]

The Hobbies

Traditional

[36]

3. The beaux, those sweet gentlemen's hobby, by heck,
   Is to wear great large poultices tied round the neck,
   And think in the tone and the tippy they're dresst,
   If they've breeches that reach from the ankle to chest. [*Refrain*]

4. The hobbies of sailors, when safe moor'd in port,
   Are their wives and their sweethearts to toy with and sport;
   When our navy's completed, their hobby shall be
   To show the whole world that America's free. [*Refrain*]

5. The Americans' hobby has long since been known;
   No tyrant or king shall from them have a throne.
   Their states are united, and let it be said
   Their hobby is Madison, peace, and free trade. [*Refrain*]

Foggy, Foggy Dew

Traditional

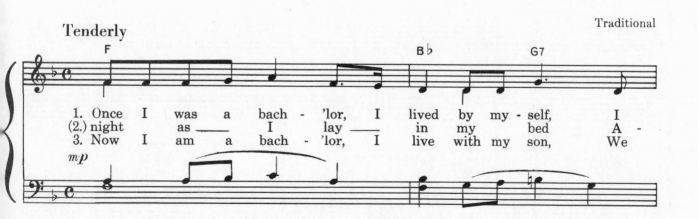

Go Tell Aunt Rhody

Traditional

Pop Goes the Weasel

Traditional

The Riddle Song

Traditional

Jefferson and Liberty

Traditional

1. The gloom - y night __ be - fore us flies, The
Eur - ope's wants __ and woes re - mote,
lord - ling here __ with gorg - ing jaws Shall

reign of ter - ror now __ is o'er. __ Its gags, in - qui - si -
friend - ly waste of waves __ be - tween, __ Here plen - ty cheers __ the
wring from in - dus - try __ the food, __ Nor fi - ery big - ot's

tors, and spies, Its herds __ of harp - ies are no more.
hum - ble lot And smiles __ on ev - ery vil - lage green.
ho - ly laws Lay waste __ our fields __ and streets in blood!

REFRAIN

Re - joice, Co - lum - bia's sons, re - joice! To ty - rants nev - er

bend — the knee, But join with heart and soul — and voice, For Jef - fer - son — and li - ber - ty.

1. 2. 3. 4.

5.

2. From — li - ber - ty. _____
3. No —

4. Here strangers from a thousand shores,
   Compelled by tyranny to roam,
   Shall find amidst abundant stores
   A nobler and a happier home. [*Refrain*]

5. Here Art shall lift her laurel'd head,
   Wealth, Industry, and Peace divine,
   And where dark, pathless forests spread,
   Rich fields and lofty cities shine. [*Refrain*]

Shenandoah

Traditional

(1816-1859)

3
EXPANSION, BY LAND AND BY SEA
(1816-1859)

Through midcentury the big thrust would be expansion. It was as if the whole country had gone from a jog to a gallop. In the North, with mass immigration supplying the muscle, industrial expansion saw factories seed the landscape and canals, railroads, and turnpikes furrow the countryside. In the South, vast expansion of the cotton trade pushed slavery to its peak. In the West, territorial expansion spurring large-scale farming and the Gold Rush spelled disaster for the Indians. And expansion by sea would find American packets, clippers, and whalers streaking across oceans with people, post, and precious cargo. From each sector there was an outpouring of song; shanties and spirituals, lullabyes and laments, dancing tunes and darn fool ditties. "Blow the Man Down!" and "Erie Canal" would come out of the North, "Blue-Tail Fly" and "Follow the Drinkin' Gourd" from the South, and "Sweet Betsy from Pike," "Hush, Little Baby," and "Skip to My Lou" from the West—a rich legacy still sung today.

With the Treaty of Ghent sealing the War of 1812, Americans were free at last to develop the territory they had won. If there was one thing everyone agreed on, it was America's manifest destiny to grow. In fulfilling it, the American dream would emerge. The nation plunged into an era of contradictions that confused materialism with idealism. On the one hand, there was the slave question precipitating the Missouri Compromise; on the other, the voice of William Lloyd Garrison pricking the American conscience with a call for emancipation. With Andrew Jackson political control soon passed from an aristocracy of education, position, and wealth to the common man. Enfranchised white males would vote in free education and banks issue loans on easy terms to farmers, small businessmen, and mechanics.

Pride in the past and abundant faith in the future nourished the American dream: the United States was the best, the biggest, and most virtuous country in the world. Among many key figures playing out this dream were statesmen Andrew Jackson, Henry Clay, and John Calhoun, Douglas, Lincoln, and Daniel Webster; inventors Hunt, Howe, Goodyear, and Morse; philosophers Emerson and Thoreau; reformers John Noyes, Sylvester Graham, and Margaret Fuller, Harriet Beecher Stowe, and John Brown; naturalist Audubon, physician Crawford Long, and physicist Joseph Henry; explorer Fremont and engineer Ezra Cornell; showmen Barnum and Bailey; the Hudson River school of painters; writers Whitman, Hawthorne, Poe, and Melville; as well as composers Gottschalk and Foster. But the hero of the day was the self-made man. Hardly an area of life was untouched by the philosophy of self-reliance as reflected in the foreign-policy stance of the Monroe Doctrine (1823).

Within little more than four decades fifteen new states would join the union, and the flag would go through as many changes, with stars fancifully arranged in circles, squares, or as one big star. Undeterred by the panics of '19, '37, and '57, the nation rolled forward. With geographical growth came phenomenal industrial development, a turning point in American history that transformed an agrarian society into an industrial one; water power, fuel and iron, immigrant labor, Yankee ingenuity and enterprise effected the change. These in tandem with westward expansion would increase demands that could only be met by inventions, some twenty-eight thousand in a period of sixty years. Shop and cottage industries gave way to factory systems with textile manufacturing completely mechanized; carpets woven by power looms; glassware, furniture, carriages and wagons, hats and shoes—all mass-produced.

In basic industry blast furnaces and rolling mills proliferated, with coal replacing charcoal in smelting. William Kelly invented a process that converted pig iron into steel and received his U.S. patent the same year as Englishman Bessemer.

With all the advances in industry there was none in labor. If low pay (five dollars a week), wretched living and working conditions were the lot of the unskilled workingman, that of the working needle-woman was far worse (fourteen to twenty-four cents a day take-home pay). Small wonder the first strike on record involving women employees occurred as early as 1824. A year later another significant strike took place when six hundred carpenters in Boston called for a ten-hour day. Farm workers fared no better than organized city craftsmen. Their average wage: about forty cents a day plus board.

If the farmer had little concern for his worker, he had even less for his land; for him it was a means to a quick fortune. The exception was the Pennsylvania Dutch farmer who still retained his Old World respect for the soil. Others sold or abandoned land they

deemed no longer profitable to exploit new areas. Those staying behind, unable to compete with grain production in the West, soon turned to poultry and dairy farming. Farmers pressing on through Illinois and Iowa conquered the tall prairie grass with black-smith John Deere's steel plow and at harvest time gathered in the wheat with Cyrus McCormick's new mechanical reaper. This was just the beginning. There would be horse- and steam-powered machinery for threshing wheat, grinding corn, processing cheese and, in the South where slaves continued to till fields with primitive tools, new machinery for refining sugar and hulling rice. With improved machinery wheat and corn farmers could now work larger fields. As productivity increased, the number of farmers would decrease, with only five out of ten Americans tied to the land by 1860. By this time too, John Norton's *Scientific Agriculture* had replaced the *Farmer's Almanac,* the first agricultural colleges opened, and mass-produced foodstuffs were a fact of life.

Along major waterways areas began to develop where farmers could bring commodities for sale or shipment. Pittsburgh, Wheeling, Marietta, Cincinnati,

Terre Haute, and St. Louis flourished as trading and processing centers. Everything from pole-propelled rafts to paddle-wheelers—the pride of major rivers—got them there. In 1825 "Clinton's Ditch" became the great Erie Canal, and in the 1840s canal travel hit its peak with a four-and-a-half-thousand-mile network. Unhurried passengers, who considered ducking bridges great sport and could afford the six dollars and the six and a half days it might take to go from Philadelphia to Pittsburgh, preferred the roll of a canal boat to the rock of a coach.

Meanwhile train travel, which by 1847 had become part of everyday life in the East, was rough on the body, unbearable to the choking point. Windows sealed in winter opened in summer, smoke and soot pouring in, hard seats and hazardous night journeys adding to the discomfort. By the end of the 1850s Henry Campbell's "American-type" locomotive, the most powerful in the world, had steamed up to the Mississippi and would cross it before the next era was done. The speed and availability of trains, plus a sharp rise in prices, soon saw freight switching from canal to rail.

For freight going out of the country there were the merchant marine's flash packets under the Black Ball and Swallow Tail flags. These would capture cargo and passenger traffic between Liverpool and New York as early as 1816. The hardships of transatlantic travel, though excruciating, would be endured by some four million immigrants with the dream of full stomachs ahead. The crews, often lured by the adventure and romance of the sea in their youth, experienced disillusionment, disenchantment, and despair, tellingly expressed in soulful shanties and Richard Dana's *Two Years Before the Mast.*

By 1848 John Griffiths had revolutionized ship design with the *Rainbow.* Old hands seeing her built claimed "her bows are turned inside out." If dismal predictions accompanied the launching of early clippers, they faded away the moment speed, not burden-bearing, spelled profit. The fleetest, most beautiful ships afloat would fast overtake the British in world trade; another fulfillment of the American dream.

With the increase of traffic in and out of the country, new foods, such as oranges and lemons, entered the American diet. Tomatoes were no longer considered poisonous, and fruits and vegetables were put up in glass jars. With Nathaniel Wyeth's ice cutter on the market, Thomas Moore's ice box (around for years) came into popular use. The concept of refrigerated railway cars, "ice boxes on wheels," arrived as early as 1842. The ice cream habit spread and dinners of fresh seafood (which had been packed in ice) could be enjoyed by affluent Midwesterners, although regular refrigerated service was to develop at a later date. The favorite beverages by the 1850s were coffee and milk, just when Gail Borden discovered how to evaporate milk and the jaws of the nation started moving up and down with the first chewing gum. By this time Americans had a reputation for eating not only too

much, but too fast. At most inns where the rule was eat all you want for 25¢, whiskey 5¢ extra; the pattern was "gobble, gulp, and go." So when the tavern-keeper's bell sounded, there was always a mad rush from washing pump to long table.

At the other end of the spectrum were people like the Reverend Sylvester Graham who extolled the virtues of flour made from whole-grain wheat (Graham flour), the value of food in its natural state, and plenty of fresh air and exercise. From his pulpit he exhorted parishoners and the world at large to swear off liquor, tobacco, tight corsets, feather beds, hot mince pie, and water with meals.

By the 1830s religion showed great diversity. It was a time of industrialization, rapidly shifting social standards, tumultuous population growth, and the opening of the West. Camp meetings flourished side by side with military musters, cabin raisings, and political barbeques—institutions already deeply woven into the fabric of America. Frontier religion, based on the literal interpretation of the Bible, was highly emotional. A number of sects arose claiming new roads to salvation, with Shakers, Millerites, and Mormons separating themselves to escape the influence of traditional faiths. Also common during this period were practitioners of mesmerism, phrenology, and psychometry, or those who would challenge reliance on religious institutions as intermediaries between man and God. The epitome of this philosophy was transcendentalism, the belief that all men

were spiritual equals and the individual conscience superior to conventional morality. American transcendentalists clustered about Concord, Massachusetts—Emerson, Hawthorne, Thoreau, and Margaret Fuller—with *The Dial* their voice, Brook Farm the embodiment of their ideals.

As writers, all contributed to a "golden age" in American literature that produced Hawthorne's *Scarlet Letter*, Melville's *Moby-Dick*, Whitman's *Leaves of Grass*, Poe's tingling tales and poems. Experimental verse forms and themes of individualism, democracy, and sectionalism made a distinctly American statement. Individualism—the "goodness" of man, the larger-than-life man—was to come through in Melville's Captain Ahab and Poe's conquering Tamerlane; democracy—the "people"—in Emerson, Thoreau, Whitman, and Whittier whose "Ichabod" rebuked Daniel Webster for supporting the Fugitive Slave Act; and sectionalism—North and South—in the legends and brooding puritanism of New England's Longfellow and Hawthorne, the southern state of mind in Longstreet, Kennedy, and Simms. American literature had its polemics too. Advocating birth control, future congressman Robert Dale Owen, with *Moral Physiology*. Equally provocative, bluestocking Margaret Fuller boldly claimed in *Woman in the Nineteenth Century* that, when it came right down to it, there really was no such thing as an entirely masculine man or an entirely feminine woman.

Feminism was on the rise. In 1848 two women, Elizabeth Stanton and Lucretia Mott, organized the first women's-rights congress in Seneca Falls, N.Y. Once Amelia Bloomer came on the scene, the women of John Noyes's Oneida community cut their hair and ran around in bloomers. Proof that women also had minds came with the opening of Mt. Holyoke College and the Boston Female Medical School. No sooner had female clerks and waitresses become a familiar sight than Elizabeth Blackwell became America's first female physician.

A few years earlier another young physician, Crawford Long, also made history when he used ether for surgery, while still another doctor, Oliver Wendell Holmes, gave the procedure its name—anesthesia. As medicine and matters of health increasingly penetrated public consciousness, homeopathy, hydropathy, and vegetarianism were to grow in popularity.

The reforming spirit, strong in nineteenth-century America, came down heavy on the side of temperance and abolitionism, with the abolitionists waging a battle of words for decades in Congress, on street corners, and in print. Following freeman Denmark Vesey's 1822 insurrection at Charleston the movement built slowly and gained momentum only after Nat Turner's revolt in 1831 had brought about more stringent slave codes. Heading the protesters in those early years were author and future congressman Owen, *Liberator* editor Garrison, and Liberty Party leader James Birney. By 1842 the Methodist and Baptist churches had both split and the North-South cleavage widened with each new territory. By the century's halfway mark, twenty thousand slaves had slipped north by Underground Railway, and the Fugitive Slave Act had passed. Abolitionist sympathies fanned by *Uncle Tom's Cabin* rose to an angry crescendo with the Dred Scott decision (Congress had no power to exclude slavery from new territories) and the slavery issue was pushed stage center by the Lincoln-Douglas debates. Then John Brown raided Harper's Ferry and two years later soldiers marched off to war singing "John Brown's Body."

A boon to all reform movements was the advance in communications. With the invention of the rotary press the United States was blanketed with newspapers, and the words *okay* and *millionaire*, coined by them, became part of everyday speech. Once painter-turned-inventor Morse had developed the telegraph, small-town papers were featuring Mexican War dispatches and headline "news by lightning wire" (1848). Soon railroads were using the telegraph for signaling, dispatching, and traffic, but it was with the winning of the West that the telegraph came into its own. Although in the early days of the Gold Rush, before the Mississippi was spanned by telegraph or railroad, the carrier of news, mail, and freshly mined gold dust was Wells Fargo, a young firm that grew up to be American Express.

Just about the time gold rushers in Colorado were gasping "Pike's Peak or Bust!" a man named Drake struck oil in Titusville, Pennsylvania. The year was 1858 and the price of whale oil sky-high. The quest for "cheap" oil had come to an end; the first American oil rush was to begin.

As oil lamps replaced spermaceti candles, more and more small heads bent over homework. By 1850 there were three and a half million pupils in eighty thousand primary schools being taught by ninety thousand teachers using McGuffey's Readers. Although secondary schools were still few, every child's right to an education was now assured—another realization of the American dream.

Informal education showed marked growth too, with the opening of more and more specialty schools and the popularity of lectures, lectures, lectures. Even factory girls attended lectures as an employee benefit, along with instruction in the domestic arts. Elias Howe was to make one domestic art easier when he patented the sewing machine, thought of years earlier

by inventor Walter Hunt, who couldn't bear the idea of putting seamstresses out of work were he to pursue the patent. Yet, believing in Manifest Destiny, Hunt could turn around and devise a repeating rifle to exterminate Indians and wild animals because that was an invention both useful and honorable! A man of his time, he later invented the safety pin, the paper collar, and circus shoes for walking up walls. The shoes were a fantastic success, as were the rolling shows of Bailey and the sideshows of Barnum; midget Tom Thumb and singer Jenny Lind made a fortune for the man who said, "There's a sucker born every minute."

By far the most popular entertainment was the minstrel show, started by four white men in blackface with fright wigs, the Virginia Minstrels. In an era that produced the American minstrel show with its distinctive music and dance, a sport was to develop that became an American institution—baseball. As early as 1858 there were twenty-five organized clubs; the game was played with underhand pitching, no gloves, fly balls caught in caps, and top-hatted umpires ignoring the difference between balls and strikes.

Interest in spectator sports, from trotting races to billiard contests, came out of growing cities where changing life-styles permitted more leisure. In New York, theaters were filled to capacity for concerts, ballets, lectures, and Shakespeare sharing bills with jugglers, acrobats, and animal acts; 50¢ bought the best seat in the house. Then as dance halls shook with the schottische, the polka, and the whirl of the waltz, Olmstead laid out Central Park and the stock exchange moved indoors off Wall Street. By this time

New York was considered the nation's rowdiest commercial city, Philadelphia the quietest, and Boston the most cultured. In the decade preceding the Civil War, large cities had streets lined with offices, saloons, and rooming houses—the poor in slums and ghettoes. They witnessed the arrival of the ward boss, the labor union, the sensational cheap press, and that curious custom, moving day. On the first of each May and October whole towns seemed to shift on their foundations as streets were filled with furniture and carts. Even houses were moved. But the newest feature on the northern landscape was the factory village with the company's sprawling mill, the owner's elegant mansion, and workers' look-alike row houses.

If the exterior of most northern homes seemed unchanged, the opposite was true of interiors with the advent of wallpaper, chintz slipcovers, and upholstered furniture, painted floor cloths and hooked rugs; Duncan Phyfe tables, Davenport desks, and Boston rockers. Plants were moved indoors (fir trees at Christmas), decorated tinware grew stylish, coffee grinders common, tubs less so, with baths forbidden without prescription in Boston, and iron ranges slowly supplanted fireplaces for cooking. Oysters stewed, fried, or *au gratin* became a passion and hams, hung in doorways for snacking, a fixture. Little girls "cooked" in toy tinware, mothered homemade dolls, struggled with samplers, or jumped rope while little boys whittled, spun tops, shot marbles or pea shooters; the new wind-up toys were the delight of all. Evenings, the whole family loved gathering round the table for the newest game—anagrams. But the gayest, most exciting diversion for village folk was the traveling circus or country fair with balloon ascensions, tightrope walkers, and horse races.

During the forties and fifties "vacationers" with brightly colored bandboxes took to the road; Niagara Falls, Saratoga Springs, and the White Mountains were popular stops. But coach travel was apt to be cramped with perfumed ladies in crinolines yards wide crushing side-whiskered gents in fitted frock coats and pants. In stark contrast were the styles of travelers heading west in the big wagons: women in poke bonnets, coarse woolen capes and dresses; long-haired, clean-shaven men in slouch hats and buckskins. The overland drive via the Oregon and Santa Fe trails was long, a good four months, and risky, especially through the desert. With the loss of horses and cattle so great, travelers walked endlessly through empty burning spaces to spare those that were left. When the mile-long caravan halted at sunset, a meal of mule meat seasoned with gunpowder was not uncommon. Much storytelling and Bible reading

around the fire renewed the faith, but the sound of a fiddle always buoyed the spirit, with the young folk breaking into a dance and everyone joining in song.

Once gold was discovered at Sutter's mill in 1848, everybody's goal became California. With the continent impassable in winter, eager gold rushers took one of two maritime routes: across Central America, with the risk of yellow fever and cholera, or around Cape Horn, a year's voyage. These people too, sang their songs, as would others a decade later when thirty-five thousand Easterners with gold fever were to flood Colorado and turn Denver into a boom town.

Although sour dough went west on every prospector's back and in every "prairie schooner," the life-

styles of the various settlers were diverse. The prairie farmer built a sod house and lived off the land; the woodsman and trapper, a log cabin or tepee-type dwelling, and survived by the gun; the miner in a crude wooden shack depended on gold dust. Quiet as was the farmer's life, the miner's was boisterous; the prairie farmer's settling down was reminiscent of the East's early settlers, and the gold digger's striking out in new directions was the force of circumstance. Most would be driven to drink, duel, or gamble by hard labor, inflated prices ($10 a dozen for eggs), a monotonous diet (bacon, flapjacks, and coffee, an occasional hunk of venison or bear meat costing its weight in gold dust), illness, and homesickness.

As Manifest Destiny was violently expanding the West and industrially transforming the North, the South, hardly touched, was standing still. Despite record yields of tobacco, turpentine, rice, sugar, and cotton, the plantation economy was headed for bankruptcy by the second half of the nineteenth century. The reasons were many: rising costs and fixed cotton prices, wealth and power controlled by large planters (a minority), small planters stymied by the lack of labor, soil abuse, and, worst of all, the slave system.

If the South was also impoverished educationally—schools few and inadequate, libraries almost nonexistent—it was culturally rich. Cities and towns sprouted choral and thespian societies, more and more theaters were built and a wider audience took in plays, concerts, and lectures. Balloon ascensions and revivals were popular with the average Southerner, but the blackface minstrel show, cutting across all class lines, was everybody's favorite, adding new dimensions to America's musical heritage with its special brand of songs and banjo "jigs" (the rhythmic source of ragtime and early jazz). One of the most popular "jigs" of the day was banjoist Dan Emmett's "Pea-Patch." A prolific composer and protean man, he played the fiddle, told jokes, sang and wrote songs. "Dixie," introduced by Bryant's Minstrels just before the Civil War, would make him famous. But Emmett made history one night in 1843 when he and three other comedians stepped onto New York's Bowery Circus stage with banjo, fiddle, tambourine, and bones (castanets). Billed as the Virginia Minstrels, they put on the very first minstrel show. Groups quickly sprang up all over the place, with the Christy Minstrels leading the pack—and no wonder, since they had a man named Foster writing for them. "Oh! Susannah," "Camptown Races," "Nelly Bly!," "Old Black Joe," minstrel hits all, never touched the popularity of "Swanee River" ("Old Folks at Home"). According to one music journal, "it's on everybody's tongue . . . pianos and guitars groan with it . . . ladies sing it . . . boatmen roar it out . . . all the bands play it." One hundred and seventy-five songs poured out of Stephen Foster in a life cut short at thirty-eight. And if genteel society looked down on minstrel music, it might hear his instrumental works in the concert hall along with those of contemporaries Fry, Heinrich, and Gottschalk. By this time a number of cities had symphony orchestras; many homes, pianos (twenty-one thousand built by 1860); and most towns, brass bands. Band concerts were a mixture of marches, quicksteps, waltzes, and polkas alternating with solos for voice and brass; the solos on keyed bugle always dazzled the audience with pyrotechnics. Bands went to camp meetings too, where they backed up the singing of white spirituals, simplified versions of folk hymns everyone could understand and sing.

Also from revivalist communities came the play-party song—"Skip to My Lou" skipping yet. Play parties, invented to circumvent church opposition to round and square dancing, saw adults adopting children's skipping, dancing, and marching movements with partners swung by the hand, never the waist. Body contact, along with the fiddle (the devil's instrument), was forbidden and in lieu of callers, lyrics cued dancers' movements—specific directions always ensuring a childlike innocence, always keeping adults a chaste distance apart. So religion, in one way or another, strongly affected the music of this period as well as social decorum.

Black spirituals, more than religious songs, were the slave's coded messages, devotional exercises, vocalized safety valves—a radical method of preserving the secrecy of criticisms and communications within a religious framework. If they relieved the ache and tedium of toil and bolstered the dream of escape, they were also the valuable record of traditions and beliefs, the soulful expression of fears and longings.

"Shouts," viewed as a religious exercise and natural expression of devotional feelings, took two forms. In one, with church benches pushed to the walls, the whole congregation might shout something like "O Lord, Remember Me" as it marched and sang—sometimes for hours. In the other, song and dance were ritualized. First three or four people stood in a circle and sang in unison. Then using a half-shuffle-half-dance step they fell into a trance, soon to be caught up in a religious frenzy that might last twenty or thirty minutes.

To survive, blacks had to be devious. Using spirituals as a code language was one way to get around The Man. It is said that Nat Turner used "Steal Away" to call co-conspirators; Harriet Tubman notified Underground Railroad candidates with "Go Down, Moses" and taught friends how to throw off the scent of bloodhounds with "Wade in the Water"; and with "Follow the Drinkin' Gourd" (the Big Dipper, north) a runaway slave could make underground connections to freedom. Then once he got there, "Good News, Member" would report by singing telegraph the joyful gospel of his safe arrival.

Another large category of spirituals was the work song. In some occupations, especially boating and railroading, the ability to sing certain songs in a certain way was a badge of membership. But whatever the

chore, there was always a spiritual. Boatmen stroked to "Michael, Row the Boat Ashore," blacksmiths hit the forge to "Hammer Ring," levee slaves loaded cotton to "Sing, Sally O," "Liza Lee," and "Shallo Brown," while female slaves spun to "Keep yo' eye on de sun, see how she run, don't let her catch you with yo' work undone." But the most exotic of work songs, and the seedling of the blues, was the one-man "holler." Usually a long, rhythmic complaint, as in the mule driver's "holler" at a baiky beast, it might be no more than a one-liner repeated over and over again. Yet still another breed of work song—"The Hog-Eye Man" and "Sacramento"—was the black shanty, part of a great body of music that billowed in packet and clipper days.

Though shanties were sung long after steam becalmed the age of sail, no new ones would develop; the need for them, tasks demanding hard physical labor, eliminated. But if sea songs decreased fatigue and increased output, the different rhythms of differ-ent tasks dictated their variety. Short-haul shanties were simple in form for short, sharp pulls; "Haul the Bowline" is one of the oldest. Halyard shanties such as "Whiskey Johnny" were for longer, heavier chores. When hoisting sail the shantyman yelled out the solo with the crew on the ropes chanting each refrain. Windlass or capstan shanties eased such long-term jobs as hoisting anchor and warping ship. In winding the rope about the capstan, the men had to walk round and round, pushing the capstan bar before them. The shanties that worked best—"Sally Brown," "A-Roving," "Stormalong," "Leave Her, Johnny, Leave Her"—had long choruses and a "swing" to them. Fore-castle songs, the songs of leisure, ran the gamut—mod-ified shanties, sentimental ditties, ballads, love songs, and nonsense tunes. Unlike the work songs, where man sang against the elements, these enjoyed the accompaniment of a fiddle or harmonica. But accom-panied or unaccompanied, there's little doubt that the nation's expansion was continually echoed in song.

Blow the Man Down!

Traditional

5. She was round in the counter and bluff in the bow,
　　To me way! Hey! Blow the man down!
So I tailed her my flipper and took her in tow.
　　Give me some time to blow the man down!

6. But as we were a-going she said unto me,
　　To me way! Hey! Blow the man down!
"There's a New York–bound rigger just ready for sea."
　　Give me some time to blow the man down!

7. But soon as that rigger was clean of the bar,
　　To me way! Hey! Blow the man down!
The mate knocked me out with the end of a spar.
　　Give me some time to blow the man down!

8. So I give you fair warning before we're away:
　　To me way! Hey! Blow the man down!
Don't never take heed of what pretty girls say.
　　Give me some time to blow the man down!

Erie Canal

Traditional

*Sung "ee-rye-ee."

[56]

Sweet Betsy from Pike

Traditional

Whimsically, not too fast

1. Oh, don't you re-mem-ber sweet Bet-sy from Pike? She crossed the big moun-tains with
2. The Shang-hai ran off, and their cat-tle all died; That morn-ing the last piece of

her lov-er Ike, With two yoke of cat-tle, a large yel-low dog,
ba-con was fried; Poor Ike was dis-cour-aged and Bet-sy got mad; The _

tall Shang-hai roos-ter, and one spot-ted hog.
dog drooped his tail and looked won-drous-ly sad.
Say-ing, "Good bye, Pike Coun-ty, fare-

well for a-while, We'll_ come back a-gain when we've panned out our pile."

3. They soon reached the desert when Betsy gave out,
And down in the sand she lay rolling about,
While Ike, half distracted, looked on with surprise,
Saying, "Betsy, get up, you'll get sand in your eyes." [Refrain]

4. Old Ike and sweet Betsy got married, of course,
But Ike in his jealousy got a divorce,
While Betsy, well satisfied, said with a smile,
"There are six good men waitin' within half a mile." [Refrain]

Buffalo Gals

Traditional

Lively

1. As I was lum-b'ring down the street, down the street, down the street, A
2. I asked her would she have some talk, have some talk, have some talk. Her

hand-some gal I chanced to meet. Oh, she was fair to view.
foot cov-ered up the whole side-walk And left no room for me.

REFRAIN

Buf-fa-lo gals, can't you come out to-night, come out to-night, come out to-night?

Buf-fa-lo gals, can't you come out to-night And dance by the light of the moon?

3. I asked her would she have a dance,
   Have a dance, have a dance.
   I thought that I might get a chance
   To shake a foot with her. [Refrain]

4. I'd like to make that gal my wife,
   Gal my wife, gal my wife.
   I'd be happy all my life,
   If I had her by me. [Refrain]

Single Girl

Sadly

Traditional

1. When I was sin-gle, go dressed neat and fine; Now I am mar-ried, go
2. When I was sin-gle, my shoes they did screak; Now I am mar-ried, my

REFRAIN

rag-ged all the time. } I wish I were a sin-gle girl a-gain, Lord, Lord; I just
shoes they al-ways leak. }

1. 2. 3. 4. 5.

6.

wish I were a sin-gle girl a-gain.

gain.

3. When I was single, I ate biscuit pie.
   Now I am married, eat cornbread or die. [Refrain]

4. Two little babies all for to retain.
   Neither one able to help me one grain. [Refrain]

5. One crying, "Mama, I want a piece of bread."
   One crying, "Mama, I want to go to bed." [Refrain]

6. Wash them and dress them and put them to bed,
   Before your man curses them and wishes you were dead. [Refrain]

Skip to My Lou

Traditional

5. Mice in the cheese crock. Chew chew chew....

6. Cat's in the cream jar. Scat, skidoo....

7. Cows in the cornfield, two by two....

8. Tripped my partner. What'll I do?...

Hush, Little Baby

Smoothly

Traditional

Follow the Drinkin' Gourd

Traditional

Wade in the Water

Nelly Bly!

Stephen C. Foster

3. Nelly Bly shuts her eye
   When she goes to sleep,
   When she wakens up again
   Her eye-balls 'gin to peep.
   De way she walks, she lifts her foot,
   And den she brings it down,
   And when it lights der's music dah
   In dat part ob de town. [*Refrain*]

4. Nelly Bly! Nelly Bly!
   Nebber, nebber sigh,
   Nebber bring de tear-drop
   To de corner ob your eye,
   For de pie is made ob punkins
   And de mush is made ob corn,
   And der's corn and punkins plenty, lub,
   A-lyin' in de barn. [*Refrain*]

Jim Crack Corn
(Blue-Tail Fly)

Traditional

3. The pony ran, he jumped and pitched,
   And tumbled Master in the ditch.
   He died; the jury wondered why:
   The verdict was the blue-tail fly. [Chorus]

4. They laid him 'neath a 'simmon tree.
   His epitaph is there to see:
   "Beneath this stone I'm forced to lie,
   All because of the blue-tail fly." [Chorus]

(1860-1865)

4

THE BLUE AND THE GRAY
(1860-1865)

In six short years America took a great fall but, unlike Humpty Dumpty, was to be put back together again. The cascade of events that began with the election of Lincoln and ended with the Thirteenth Amendment saw one nation become two struggle through civil war—the bloodiest war in American history—and expand to distant corners of the continent.

Folk songs have always flourished in periods of upheaval and the Civil War period was no exception. People trekking west sang "Shoot the Buffalo"; those settling on the prairie, "Little Old Sod Shanty"; farmers finding rich land, silver, and gold, "The Promised Land." In the East every battle inspired songs. "Maryland! My Maryland!" came out of Antietam, "On to Richmond!," the Seven Days' Fight; "Roll, Alabama, Roll," a naval encounter; "Sherman's March to the Sea," the smell of victory. And black regiments, America's first, sang freedom songs: "O, Freedom!," "Many Thousand Go," "Song of the Freedman." "Dixie" belonged to the South and "John Brown's Body" to the North, but both shared "Tenting Tonight."

A crumbling union, one-eighth slaves, weighed heavily on mens' souls as they went to the polls in 1860; each vote was highly charged with emotion, deeply rooted in conviction. Everyone knew that if Lincoln won, with the North determined to preserve the union and the South the status quo, war was inevitable. In a matter of weeks South Carolina was to toss the first stone by seceding. Then to keep another state (California) *in* the Union, the Pony Express ran between St. Jo, Missouri, and Sacramento; one of its riders was teen-aged Bill Cody, later known as Buffalo Bill. With transportation ever improving and distribution of foodstuffs more widespread, five million cans of milk, fruits, and vegetables were put up that year. At Christmas, there were shrieks of joy as children unwrapped toys with moving figures and bells.

Early in the new year Kansas joined the Union as a free state and, before Lincoln's inaugural, six more states dropped out to form the Confederacy under Jefferson Davis. By April 12 southern batteries had fired on Fort Sumter. The Civil War was on its bloody way. Within the week Lincoln retaliated with a ring of ships around southern ports. Soon after that, the Confederacy swelled to eleven states and moved its capital to Richmond.

This was also the year that steel production moved into high, modernizing warfare and weaponry. Armed with one of the new weapons was a private, Kady Brownell, who fought alongside her husband at Bull Run. The war spirit caught by another woman, militant suffragette Julia Ward Howe, found expression in "Battle Hymn of the Republic"—a bestselling broadside in factory, field, and camp. The recent development of cheap newsprint saw cities and towns literally papered with broadsides. But just as the local broadside was left far behind, the Pony Express was stopped in its tracks by the first coast-to-coast telegram crackling over the wires from Sacramento to the White House.

Although the Pony Express was no more, the westward movement continued unabated—and with government help; the '62 Congress legislated expansion with the Homestead Act and granted thirty thousand acres per state for agricultural and mechanical schools. Out of the same session came antipolygamy measures; soon after, Miss Lavinia Warren, thirty-two inches tall, married "General" Tom Thumb, who towered eight inches above her, in a fashionable wedding in New York. There, and in other fashion-conscious cities, men were wearing beards, melon-shaped hats (derbies), sack coats, detachable collars and cuffs, trousers in checks and plaids. Women, the butts of many a caricature, wore flowerpot hats and ridiculously belled skirts over hoop cages so wide they left their mark on many a doorframe. Yards and yards of tulle or mousseline made them walking fire hazards. Mrs. Longfellow, the poet's wife, was to burn to death sealing a letter with wax!

On June 1, 1862, Robert E. Lee took command of Confederate forces and three months later led them into Antietam, the bloodiest battle of the war, where they were checked by General McClellan. But by December, Lee had vindicated himself with victory at Fredericksburg. And while all this was going on, a young artist on assignment from *Harper's Weekly* was quietly sketching the war in Union camps; his name— Winslow Homer. Another artist on the battlefield—the camera, not the pencil, his tool—was Matthew Brady.

On New Year's Day 1863 the president issued his Emancipation Proclamation. For the North it marked a turning point in the war. The conflict was now a crusade for freedom. Lincoln's call for three hundred thousand more men may have inspired a song, "We Are Coming, Father Abraham," but not many volunteers. So in March, the first Conscription Act went into effect, with well-heeled draftees buying substitutes for three hundred dollars. This inequity would not go unchallenged. During the hot summer antidraft riots erupted costing over one thousand lives and one and a half million dollars in damage. The South's solution to the manpower shortage was to urge the enlistment of slave soldiers, provided both slave and owner volunteered.

Food production was in need of boosting too. Unquestionably, 493 patents for agricultural inventions (twice that of military) eased the way for increased yields. Another invention that year was Ebenezer Butterick's paper dress-pattern; coming at a time when children started roller skating and West Virginia joined the Union.

But there would be no celebrations on the Fourth of July, the Battle of Gettysburg ended in heartbreak —the losses of teen-age soldiers so great. These soldiers would not be forgotten for, as Lincoln so eloquently said, they had not "died in vain." Yet the war dragged on. The Chattanooga campaign around Thanksgiving, 1863, ended in a Union victory that was to make General Ulysses Grant commander-in-chief of Federal forces after the first of the next year. Off shore, the Confederates launched the first successful submarine attack. In both armies and both navies black soldiers and sailors distinguished themselves. For his part in the duel between the *Kearsage* and the *Alabama*, black sailor Joachim Pease was awarded the Congressional Medal of Honor.

Despite the war, the railroad system continued to develop without interruption. The first freight run connected Boston and Chicago; postal cars were added and sleeping cars under construction by Pullman. Cotton thread was being manufactured for the first time, croquet came to Brooklyn, the best cut of beef cost thirty cents a pound, and taxes were *up*, again.

Down south, Sherman blazed his way to Atlanta and marched on to Savannah, capturing it just before Christmas, 1864. By the end of that year the flag had thirty-six stars, the newest for the state of Nevada. At the president's insistence, stars for rebel states had remained on the flag throughout the conflict.

No sooner had Lincoln been sworn in for a second term than the crusade for freedom accelerated. Sheridan routed the rebels at Five Forks, Sherman marched to the sea, and Lee, without consulting Davis, surrendered to Grant on April 9, 1865, at Appomattox. Less than a week later, Abraham Lincoln was dead at the hand of John Wilkes Booth, the first to assassinate an American president. Once the country had pulled itself out of mourning, wild celebrations broke out from sea to shining sea. For months, some cities had balls every night (New York had six hundred) with gents in flying tails whirling voluminously skirted ladies, their eyes a-flutter with the new mascara.

Further cause for celebration was the triumph over slavery with the adoption of the Thirteenth Amend-

ment; soon black lawyer John Rock was practicing before the Supreme Court and blacks Charles Mitchell and Edward Walker were elected to a northern legislature. Ironically, South Carolina, the first state to secede, was the first southern state to free its slaves. Each a historic breakthrough, and each to be quickly blunted, by an emerging Ku Klux Klan in Tennessee.

The hatred and intolerance intensified by the war were long to remain, as were the miseries stemming from the South's sustained suffering during four long years. Starting behind, never to catch up, the end had to be ruin, with industries sparse, communications poor, transportation bad, manpower drained. For southern women, the war turned into a revolution the moment they took over plantations and converted cotton production to food production, revived household industries—spinning, weaving, and dyeing—secured paying jobs, traveled unescorted, were intellectually and socially on their own. "Making do" or "doing without" affected everybody and everything: work, play; food, shelter, and clothing; children and adults, rich and poor. There may have been shortages, but resourcefulness was never in short supply.

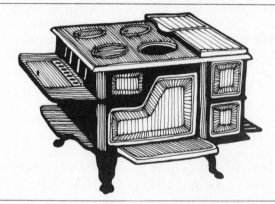

Meat-starved Southerners ate eggs ("100 Ways of Cooking an Egg"—no joke), fish, or fowl. One Louisiana father was to wake his girls with "Fish or no breakfast!" Newspaper readers were urged to eat frogs, young crows, even rats ($2.50 each as Vicksburg fell). Serious salt shortages found women on the coast boiling sea water to get the salty residue, then rolled and pulverized by children; inland, people scraped the brine off old barrels and troughs. A substitute for butter and lard was sunflower oil, a health food today. Syrupy sorghum doubtless was the basis for complaints that Confederate "ginger snaps," containing no sugar and no ginger, had very little snap. Flour (by spring '65, $1200 a barrel!—rare enough for a gift) called for a "biscuit party." But rice flour made perfectly good "rebel bread." Sage, holly, and blackberry leaves were brewed for ersatz tea; yams, pea-

nuts, and watermelon or okra seeds yielded "coffee." Since the source of most brandy was highly questionable, more than one insurance company refused to insure those who drank it; whiskey, by far the most popular beverage, was likely to be distilled from anything and everything. At "starvation parties," with only water and good fellowship on the menu, conversation was apt to be liberally larded with tidbits about tasty dishes of bygone days.

Whether they could afford it or not, families fed and housed passing armies. In caring for the wounded, the woods became their drugstore, providing dogwood berry for malaria; turpentine extract for fevers, colds, or sore throats; mustard seed for pneumonia and pleurisy.

With the housing shortage so acute in towns and rural areas near camps, refugees and camp followers, soldiers' families, and speculators commandeered empty factories, schools, and public buildings, boats, boxcars, even caves. Heating and lighting, problems too, saw green-pine prices rocket out of sight. Beds were scarce (pallets more likely); cut-up carpets became blankets (woven moss along the coast); gourds, cups; and the lowly bucket, a cherished item.

The scarcest clothing item was shoes; wood and cloth were clumsy substitutes for leather. Old clothing made over or cut down for children was worn ragged; new clothing came from sheets, curtains, or upholstery, if one was lucky; from homespun, if industrious; and from meal bags, if poor. Hairpins were straightened and oiled after each use; hair ribbons were replaced by corn shucks, smooth faces by bearded ones, chewing tobacco by rosin.

If schools without paper, pencils, books, or slates caused little distress, a world without valentines, parties, and Christmas toys broke little hearts. Rags and nuts became makings for dolls; corncobs and pasteboard for cannons and forts. But bark, berry, and root gathering (for dyes), knitting or crocheting, plaiting straw or wicker always came before play.

With diversions few, a parade was a happening at the roll of a drum, a banner across Main Street, a bazaar (the social function furthering "The Cause"), a fiddler's tune, a call to sing, swing your partner or dance at a "soldier bee." In social circles numerous entertainments were provided by the soldiers themselves—tournaments, pistol shootings, sham battles, and military balls. Women, meanwhile, provided promenades, picnics, street receptions, and amateur theatricals. Officers in northern Virginia, encouraged by General Lee, galloped into town night after night to dine and dance, riding back to camp just in time for reveille.

If the South was full of contradictions, other sections were too. On the dark side were the border states —Maryland, Delaware, Kentucky, and Missouri— where shifting tides of occupation left wakes of destruction and divided loyalties (father fighting son, neighbor killing neighbor). On the light side, grotesque in contrast, were the cities of Cincinnati and St. Louis, two veritable islands of lighthearted luxury smack in the middle of the country.

In spirit, those midwestern cities were very close to many in the North where the burden of war fell lightly on the civilian, compared to the soldier. Social functions continued as before with society wintering in town and summering in Newport, Saratoga, or on Long Island. They turned out *en masse* to hear Adelina Patti sing and applaud the bravura theatrics of Edwin Forrest and Mrs. John Drew. Minstrel shows (everybody loved them) played to standing room only, as did Gilmore's Band. On the road circuses were traveling in all directions. One summer, four passed through New Haven alone.

Spectator sports gained all the time; bare-fisted boxing teams crowd-collectors in the country, prize fights popular in the city (despite the absence of the so-called refined element). In championship matches, a new vogue, billiards were played before hundreds ($1000 a side), chess moves carried by telegraph. Baseball, fast becoming America's favorite sport, filled ball parks to capacity, as did the horse racing revival an increasing number of tracks.

As in sports, so it went in art and literature. For art it was a transitional period. With photography altering everyone's perspective, there was something new: mass-produced art at popular prices. Even modest homes had Currier and Ives prints on the walls. Most northern writers of the previous period continued to publish, many adding to the huge body of war literature. Whitman was to write his incomparable war sketches while serving as a male nurse. James Russell Lowell's latest *Biglow Papers* made people laugh. But the common touch that had brought prosperity to the art trade came to books in the form of the dime novel that "reflected the healthy state of American morals and the deplorable state of American taste."

The healthy state of American industry in the northeastern and central states not only allowed most Northerners to lead near-peacetime lives but was to be the major factor in winning the war. At the opening of hostilities, existing factories and workshops (easily converted for military use) stood ready to equip armies and replace the wastes of war; steel production was ahead of Europe by 1865. Taxes favoring larger industry saw businesses consolidating and military needs forcing the centralization of separate railroads into trunk systems. During the conflict civilian industries continued to produce steamships, locomotives, mill and power tools, textiles, paper and glass for domestic as well as foreign consumption—South America and Europe! Small wonder the daily lives of most Northerners flowed on with nary a ripple; if anything, life improved. A sure sign of prosperity would be the opening of fifteen privately endowed colleges: among them, Bates, Cornell, M.I.T., Swarthmore, and Vassar.

That Vassar opened during wartime and coincided with the emergence of some important female figures was no accident; seeds rooted in the period before the reform movement. By war's end there were three hundred women doctors, two of them eminent: Dr. Elizabeth Blackwell, founder of the New York Infirmary for Women and Children (still in existence), and Dr. Mary Walker who abandoned her practice to nurse Union soldiers at the front. Superintendent of nurses for the army was a woman noted for reforming the treatment of the insane, Dorthea Dix. A founder of the American Red Cross, Clara Barton, set up the register of missing men at Annapolis and went south in 1865 to identify graves at Andersonville. Another woman heading south after the war, Elizabeth Hyde Botume, was to establish a freedman's school in Beaufort, South Carolina, using "The Freedman's Book," a tract written by abolitionist L. Maria Child, while *Hospital Sketches* (letters of a young war worker to her family) came from the hand of a woman who'd become world famous, Louisa May Alcott. But the average northern woman, busy as she was with house and family, always found time for war work. At the local aid society she made army uniforms and hospital garments, rolled bandages, packed lint, and wrapped parcels. Those with loved ones at the front may have had lonely moments, but they never needed be alone.

The loneliness experienced by women in early homestead days—wolves, fires, and locusts notwithstanding—was more of a trial than all the work put together. The isolation of cabin life worked a terrible hardship; being left for days, even weeks, while mates went to the mill, to town, or to work. On the plains, where the wind blew day in and day out, women tended to become nervous and irritable; filthy dust filtered into everything, including their hair. While children ran about in sack garments, their mothers planted pumpkins, squashes, watermelons, muskmelons, and row upon row of cucumbers for putting up forty-gallon barrels of pickles each fall. The makeshift furnishings of a harsh life-style saw nail kegs or trunks used for chairs, boxes for tables. To make room for family activities, tables and "knocked down" beds had to be set outside, because sod houses were so small. And sod roofs that dripped after each rain meant clothes had to be stored elsewhere, usually in covered wagons. With circumstance dictating the homesteader's diet, emphasis was on quantity, not variety. In Kansas, Minnesota, and Nebraska, where the staple was corn and johnny cake the staff of life, white bread and biscuits were delicacies. Hogs supplied meat the year round, but the monotony of pork was broken by fish (from Minnesota's lakes) or a sprinkling of game. Sorghum, the sugar of the plains, converted into molasses at the local mill, sweetened everything from coffee to preserves. Wild fruits, particularly plums, gathered along streams were preserved in barrels of spring water. But limitations, inherent to pioneering, applied to fun as well as food; singing around the fire and "play parties" were about it.

For pioneers roaming the open range, singing around the fire, more than a diversion, was a cushion against loneliness. In the decade or so before the war, groups of young Americans had drifted into Texas on the heels of fleeing Mexicans who had left behind half a million wandering cattle. Rounding up the animals into corrals, later herding them north—they were America's first cowboys. By the 1860s beef-on-the-hoof had made many Texans rich; goods were plentiful—luxuries imported via Mexico. But in 1865 the Civil War that had seemed so remote from Texas was suddenly at its door. The reaction of many, cowboys included, was to move farther west.

Some three hundred thousand pioneers crossed the plains during the war, a small minority to evade the draft, to desert, or, as in the case of Mark Twain (who served a few inglorious weeks in the Confederate army), to put distance between himself and the battlefield. For the majority, it meant a fresh start. Lured by free land, lumber, silver, and gold, they settled the new territories of Dakota, Colorado, and Nevada, the states of California and Oregon, and the whole Pacific slope.

To get there, every mode of transport was pressed into service. Military priorities and the crush of civilian travel were to tax stage lines beyond limits. Probably the most colorful stage driver to cross dangerous terrain at breakneck speed and to out-drink everyone on payday was One-Eyed Charlie Pankhurst whose death revealed "he" had been a she! Then there were the big wagon trains stretching for miles, setting up tent cities at dusk (disappearing at dawn), plodding slowly onward through the vast prairie. Railroad trains, filled to capacity, went only so far as Nebraska: the laying of track for the final link to California— westward from Omaha, eastward from Sacramento— started in 1861, the result of government bonds. Boats too, filled to overflowing, steamed both sea routes from coast to coast.

The outbreak of civil war, rather than interrupting, created conditions permitting the West Coast to develop its full potential. While heavy federal wartime spending was to depreciate paper currency, the value of silver and gold mounted steadily. By cutting off the West from eastern factories, the war forced western industrialization, making the region self-sustaining. In towns from San Diego to Puget Sound, foundries, machine shops, mills, and factories proliferated, answering ever growing demands. San Francisco was rebuilt and by 1863 had more than two hundred schools, twelve daily newspapers, forty-one churches, twenty-six theaters, more than two hundred bars. The Coast, now secure in its prosperity, was ready to take sides in the conflict. Convinced that Union victory lay ahead, and for reasons more economic than ideologic, the West finally took sides and committed itself to the North in 1864.

As for the war itself, the development of heavy hardware catapulted warfare right into the modern age. With machines and their tactical uses creating a distance between men, military technology cut down the incidence of close-range combat forever. The war introduced the tactical use of the railway for troop transport and armored defense. For reconnaissance, the offshore calcium light and balloons aloft with telegraphic transmitters directed gunfire and cameras photographed enemy emplacements. Both techniques had much to do with, in fact were crucial to, the winning of the battles of Richmond and Fredericksburg. Throughout the war, considerable experimentation on both sides led to innovations and refinements in weaponry that revolutionized the character of warfare: machine guns, heavy cannon, grenades, flamethrowers; land and sea mines, submarines, electrically exploded torpedoes. The first ironclads, the *Monitor* and the *Merrimac* (equipped with revolving turrets),

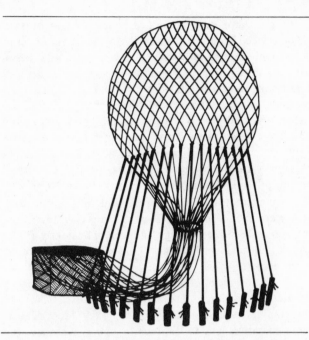

were to alter the course of naval warfare. Although application of new weaponry was not widespread (the Civil War primarily an infantryman's war), the existence of huge northern mills capable of producing better and cheaper steel made it possible. In Massachusetts, the Springfield arsenal was turning out twenty-five thousand small arms a month by 1863.

During four years of war, two thousand combats were waged, one hundred and fifty major battles fought: the cost to the North, five billion dollars; to the South, total economic ruin; to the nation, six hundred thousand men. The tragedy of this war was that both sides lost far more men from illness and bad health than from hostile bullets. The causes were many: ignorance of disease (cause and effect), poor sanitation and diet, inadequate shelter and clothing.

Based on U.S. Army Regulations of 1857, uniforms in North and South were very similar; the principal differences—head gear; cut and color of coats; the unavailability of indigo in the South, changing the prescribed blue to gray. With uniforms in both armies produced in a limited size range, much trying on and trading was necessary before recruits found even a semblance of fit. For major alterations, garments were sent home; minor ones done by the soldier himself with a sewing kit affectionately called "the housewife." Families also provided suspenders (not government issued) and, in some cases, newly patented armored vests, soon discarded. The scarcity of shoes in both sectors, infinitely worse in the South, posed serious problems; the thousands of shoeless in Lee's army was a primary cause for stragglers following each campaign.

One of the first things a new recruit did after drawing his uniform and equipment was to pay a visit to the "Daguerrian Artist" to have his "likeness" taken; the cost, one to eight dollars, a goodly portion of his monthly pay, eleven to thirteen dollars. Another way the soldier spent his money was in the PX of the day, the sutler's shop. For cakes, pies, pickles, sardines, cranberry sauce ($1.50 a can) and other delicacies he paid fancy prices, too fancy for the average soldier.

If rations were more abundant than for previous soldiers in history, they strayed little from the staples of meat and bread. Pork or beef was fresh, cured, or pickled, and the fresh was often rancid. Pork was called "sow belly" and the pickled beef, so briney it was almost inedible, "salt horse." In the North, seabiscuit or "hardtack" marked with the letters BC for Brigade Commissary ("Before Christ" according to the men) was hard, stale, and moldy. In the South, cornbread. And everywhere, of course, beans: white or army for Federals, black-eyed or speckled for Confederates. Foraging talents (particularly in the South) supplied variety—stolen sweet potatoes and unshucked corn a real treat when roasted in open fires. Coffee, imbibed by the gallon up north, was next to unobtainable down south, as was food for Confederates on the march.

Because battles were infrequent and few longer than two or three days, troops had plenty of time for games, sports, and all sorts of diversion. With easy access to books and papers, reading was popular: in the North, Frank Leslie's picture paper, the *Atlantic* and *Harper's*; *Southern Illustrated News* and *Field and Fireside* in the South; the book most widely read, north and south, the Bible. Entertainments most roundly applauded were itinerant minstrel shows and skits satirizing camp routines (rations, officers, surgeons). Sports most practiced were boxing, foot races, broad jumping, and free-for-all scuffles, with whole regiments participating in snowball fights. A much favored, yet frowned upon, diversion was gambling—notably on payday. Favored games were poker, twenty-one, keno, and faro. Soldiers steeped in midcentury orthodoxy, and fearful of being struck down with the instruments of sin on their persons, always threw cards away when advancing in battle. Once the smoke had cleared, survivors were frequently seen scurrying about recovering their discarded treasures.

But best loved by far was music, especially singing. Favorites of the Federals were "John Brown's Body," "The Battle Cry of Freedom," "Take Your Gun and Go, John," and, for comic relief, "Shoo, Fly, Shoo" and "The Captain's Whiskers." An example of southern humor was "Goober Peas," making fun of peanut-loving troops held in low esteem. More serious, more stirring numbers were "Dixie," "The Bonnie Blue Flag," "God Save the South," and in the Southwest "The Yellow Rose of Texas." In both armies black regiments had their spirituals and freedom songs, heard for the first time by many white comrades-in-arms. Sometimes the Blue and the Gray sang to each other. One southern lieutenant, writing home, said: "We are on one side of the Rappahannock, the Enemy on the other. . . . Our boys will sing a Southern song. The Yankees will reply by singing the same tune to Yankee words." And occasionally, opposing soldiers even joined in a rendition of "Tenting Tonight." Once, according to reports, when opposing bands were to take turns playing patriotic airs and one started "Home Sweet Home," the other joined in immediately and hundreds of voices from both sides united in song.

"Lorena," "The Girl I Left Behind," and "When This Cruel War Is Over" were popular with everybody—soldier and civilian alike—as were such regional hits as "The Ship That Never Returned" and "Marching Through Georgia" by abolitionist Henry Clay Work or "Tramp! Tramp! Tramp!" and "Just Before the Battle, Mother" by George Root. Of course the broadside tradition went on; the scarcity of paper limited output below the Mason-Dixon Line, but not humor, with "Lincoln on a Rail" mocking Union leaders. Other major themes were flag-waving, high courage, and God. Categories of some northern broadsides were current events ("The Draft Is A-Coming"), historic events ("Oil on the Brain"), humor ("Mickey's Dead-Broke at the Door").

Songs being sung in the Midwest, Southwest, and Far West were old ones people had brought with them, new ones that were topical and regional; the accompaniment a jaw's harp, harmonica, or fiddle, a rare piano or organ, or nothing at all. Musically, the East differed little from the previous period but not so the South, where orchestras dramatically dwindled to lone fiddlers.

Dixie

Don Emmett

[76]

CHORUS

way! Look a-way, Dix-ie Land! *f* Den I wish I was in
way! Look a-way, Dix-ie Land!
way! Look a-way, Dix-ie Land!

Dix-ie. Hoo-ray! Hoo-ray! In Dix-ie Land I'll take my stand, To

lib and die in Dix-ie, A-way, a-way, a-way down south in

Dix-ie, A-way, a-way, a-way down south in Dix-ie.

4. Now here's a health to the next old Missus,
   An' all de gals dat want to kiss us.
       Look away! Look away! Look away, Dixie Land!
   But if you want to drive 'way sorrow,
   Come and hear dis song tomorrow.
       Look away! Look away! Look away, Dixie Land! [Chorus]
5. Dar's buckwheat cakes an' Injun batter,
   Makes you fat or a little fatter.
       Look away! Look away! Look away, Dixie Land!
   Den hoe it down and scratch your grabble,
   To Dixie's land I'm bound to trabble.
       Look away! Look away! Look away, Dixie Land! [Chorus]

The Homespun Dress

Traditional

Joyfully

1. Oh, yes, I am a south-ern girl, And glo-ry in the name, _____ And boast it with far great-er pride Than glit-t'ring wealth or fame. _____ I en-vy not the north-ern girl Her robes of beau-ty rare, _____ Though dia-monds grace her snow-y neck And pearls be-deck her

2. Our home-spun dress is plain, we know, Our hat's pal-met-to, too, _____ But then, it shows what south ern girls For south-ern rights will do. _____ We scorn to wear a bit of silk Or an-y north-ern lace; _____ We make our home-spun dress-es up And wear them with a

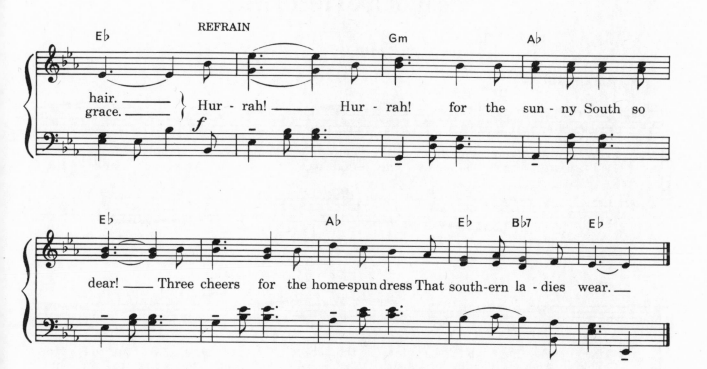

hair. ———
grace. ——— Hur - rah! ——— Hur - rah! for the sun - ny South so

dear! ——— Three cheers for the home-spun dress That south-ern la - dies wear. ———

3. Now northern goods are out of date,
   And since old Abe's blockade,
   We southern girls can be content
   With goods we Suthrons made.
   We've sent the bravest of our land
   To battle with the foe.
   So we will lend a helping hand
   To save the South we know. [*Refrain*]

4. The southern land's a glorious land
   And has a glorious cause.
   Three cheers, three cheers, for southern rights
   And for the southern boys!
   We've sent our sweethearts to the war,
   But, dear girls, never mind;
   Your soldier boy will ne'er forget
   The girl he left behind. [*Refrain*]

5. The soldier is the lad for me,
   A brave heart I adore,
   And when the sunny South is free
   And fighting is no more,
   I'll choose me then a lover brave
   From out that gallant band.
   The soldier lad I love the best
   Shall have my heart and hand. [*Refrain*]

6. And now, young lad, a word to you:
   If you would win the fair,
   Go to the field where honor calls
   And win your lassie there!
   Remember that our brightest smiles
   Are for the true and brave
   And that our tears are saved for him
   Who fills a soldier's grave. [*Refrain*]

Song of the Freedmen

Traditional

We are com - ing from the cot - ton fields, We're com - ing from a -
We will leave our chains be - hind us, boys, The pris - on and the

far; We have left the plow, the hoe, the axe, And we are off to
rack; And we'll hide be - neath a sol - dier's coat The scars up - on our

war. We have left the old plan - ta - tion seat, The sug - ar and the
back; And we'll teach the world a les - son, soon, If tak - en by the

cane, Where we worked and toiled with wea - ry feet In sun and wind and rain.
hand, How night shall come be - fore it's noon Up - on old Phar - aoh's land.

REFRAIN

Goober Peas

Traditional

With a swing

1. Sit - ting by the road - side, on a sum-mer's day,
2. When a horse-man pass - es, the sol - diers have a rule, They
3. Just be - fore the bat - tle, the gen - 'ral hears a row; He

Chat - ting with my mess - mates, pass - ing time a - way;
cry out at their loud - est, "Mis - ter, where's your mule?"
says, "The Yanks are com - ing, I hear their ri - fles now." He

Ly - ing in the sha - dow un - der - neath the trees,
But an - oth - er plea - sure, en - chant - ing more than these, Is
turns a - round in won - der, and won - ders what he sees: The

Good-ness, how de - li - cious, eat - ing goo - ber peas.
wear - ing out your grind - ers, eat - ing goo - ber peas.
Geor - gia mi - li - tia eat - ing goo - ber peas.

REFRAIN

Peas, peas, peas, peas,

eat - ing goo - ber peas; Good-ness, how de - li - cious, eat - ing goo - ber peas.

Many Thousand Go

Triumphantly

Traditional

1. No more peck o' corn for me, No more, no more;
3. No more pint o' salt for me, No more, no more;
5. No more mis - tress' call for me, No more, no more;

No more peck o' corn for me. Man - y thou - sand go.
No more pint o' salt for me. Man - y thou - sand go.
No more mis - tress' call for me. Man - y thou - sand go.

2. No more driv - er's lash for me, No more, no more;
4. No more hun - dred lash for me, No more, no more;
6. No more auc - tion block for me, No more, no more;

No more driv - er's lash for me. Man - y thou - sand go.
No more hun - dred lash for me. Man - y thou - sand go.
No more auc - tion block for me. Man - y thou - sand go.

John Brown's Body

Traditional

Militantly

1. John Brown's body lies a-mould'ring in the grave,
gone to be a soldier in the army of the Lord! He is
3. John Brown's knap-sack is strapped up-on his back,

John Brown's body lies a-mould'ring in the grave,
gone to be a soldier in the army of the Lord! He's
John Brown's knap-sack is strapped up-on his back,

John Brown's body lies a-mould'ring in the grave. His
gone to be a soldier in the army of the Lord! His
John Brown's knap-sack is strapped up-on his back. His

soul is march-ing on!
soul is march-ing on!
soul is march-ing on!

CHORUS

gradually louder and louder

B♭ *legato*

f

Glo - ry, glo - ry, hal - le - lu - jah!

E♭   B♭

Glo - ry, glo - ry, hal - le - lu - jah!

Gm   B 7   Cm   C

Glo - ry, glo - ry, hal - le - lu - jah! His soul is

fff

B♭   F   1. 2. B♭   B♭+   E♭   B♭maj7   3. B♭

mf

march - ing on! _____ 2. He's on! _____

Tenting Tonight

Walter Kittredge

[86]

3. The lone wife kneels and prays with a sigh
   That God his watch will keep
   O'er the dear one away and the little dears nigh,
   In the trundle bed fast asleep. [*Chorus*]

4. We are tenting tonight on the old camp ground.
   The fires are flickering low.
   Still are the sleepers that lie around,
   As the sentinels come and go. [*Chorus*]

5. Alas for those comrades of days gone by
   Whose forms are missed tonight.
   Alas for the young and true who lie
   Where the battle flag braved the fight. [*Chorus*]

6. No more on march or field of strife
   Shall they lie so tired and worn,
   Nor rouse again to hope and life
   When the sound of drums beat at morn. [*Chorus*]

7. We are tired of war on the old camp ground.
   Many are dead and gone
   Of the brave and true who've left their homes;
   Others been wounded long. [*Chorus*]

8. We've been fighting today on the old camp ground.
   Many are lying near:
   Some are dead and some are dying;
   Many are in tears. [*Chorus*]

When This Cruel War Is Over

3. If amid the din of battle
   Nobly you should fall,
   Far away from those that love you,
   None to hear you call—
   Who would whisper words of comfort,
   Who would soothe your pain?
   Ah! the many cruel fancies
   Ever in my brain. [*Refrain*]

4. But our country called you, darling,
   Angels cheer your way;
   While our nation's sons are fighting,
   We can only pray.
   Nobly strike for God and liberty,
   Let all nations see
   How we love the starry banner,
   Emblem of the free. [*Refrain*]

Lorena

Words by *Rev. H.D.L. Webster*
Music by *J.P. Webster*

1. The years creep slow-ly by, Lo-re-na; The
2. A hun-dred months have passed, Lo-re-na, Since
3. We loved each oth-er then, Lo-re-na, More

snow is on the grass a-gain. The sun's low down the sky, Lo-
last I held that hand in mine And felt the pulse beat fast, Lo-
than we ev-er dared to tell, And what we might have been, Lo-

re-na; The frost gleams where the flow'rs have been. But the
re-na, Though mine beat fast-er far, than thine. But
re-na, Had but our lov-ings pros-pered well. But

heart throbs on as warm-ly now As when the sum-mer days were
hun-dred months, 'twas flow-'ry May When up the hill-y slope we
then, 'tis past; the years are gone. I'll not call up their shad-'wy

4. The story of that past, Lorena,
   Alas! I care not to repeat.
   The hopes that could not last, Lorena,
   They lived, but only lived to cheat.
   I would not cause e'en one regret
   To rankle in your bosom now,
   For "If we try, we may forget"
   Were words of thine, long years ago.
       For "If we try, we may forget"
       Were words of thine, long years ago.

5. It matters little now, Lorena;
   The past is in th' eternal Past.
   Our heads will soon lie low, Lorena;
   Life's tide is ebbing out so fast.
   There is a future! Oh, thank God!
   Of life, this is so small a part!
   'Tis dust to dust beneath the sod,
   But there, up there, 'tis heart to heart.
       'Tis dust to dust beneath the sod,
       But there, up there, 'tis heart to heart.

The Ship That Never Returned

Henry C. Work

3. Said a weak young lad to his aged mother,
"I must sail that deep blue sea,
For I hear of a land in a far-off country,
Where there's health and strength for me." [*Chorus*]

4. " 'Tis a gleam of hope," said this weak young laddie,
As he kissed his weeping wife.
"Could be I'll return with a real fat purse
That will last us all through life." [*Chorus*]

Little Old Sod Shanty

Traditional

1. I'm look - in' kind - a seed - y now while head - in' down my claim; My
2. I rath - er like the nov - el - ty of liv - ing in this way, Though my

vit - tles are not al - ways of the best, _____ And the
bill of fare is nev - er of the best, _____ But I'm

mice play shy - ly round me as I nes - tle down to rest in my
hap - py as a clam ___ on the land of Un - cle Sam in my

lit - tle old sod shan - ty on the plain. _____
lit - tle old sod shan - ty in the West. _____

[Chorus]

Oh, the hing - es are of

leath-er and the win-dows have no glass; The boards let the howl-ing bliz-zard in. _____ You can see the hun-gry coy-ote As he sneaks up through the grass To my lit-tle old sod shan-ty on my claim. _____

3. When I left my eastern home a bachelor so gay
   To try to win my way to wealth and fame,
   Oh, I little thought I'd come down to burning twisted hay
   In my little old sod shanty on my claim. [*Chorus*]

4. Still I wish some kindhearted girl would pity on me take
   And relieve me from this mess that I am in.
   Oh, the angel, how I'd bless her, if this her home she'd make,
   In the little old sod shanty on my claim. [*Chorus*]

Shoot the Buffalo

Traditional

Hangtown Gals

Traditional

Lustily

1. Hang-town gals are plump and ros-y, Hair in ring-lets, might-y cos-y,
2. Dread-ful shy of val-en-tin-ers, Turn their nos-es up at min-ers,

Paint-ed cheeks and jos-sy bon-nets. Touch them and they'll sting like hor-nets.
Shocked to hear them say "Gol-durn it," Try to blush but can-not turn it.

CHORUS

Hang-town gals are love-ly crea-tures, Think they'll mar-ry Mor-mon preach-ers;

Heads thrown back to show their fea-tures. Ha, ha, ha, those Hang-town gals!

3. On the street they're always grinnin';
Modestly they lift their linen,
Petticoats all trimmed with laces,
Matching well their painted faces. [*Chorus*]

4. To church they very seldom venture;
Hoops so large they cannot enter.
Go it, gals, you're young and tender;
Shun the pick-and-shovel gender. [*Chorus*]

I Am Bound for the Promised Land

Moving forward

Traditional

1. On Jor-dan's storm-y banks I stand And cast a wish-ful eye To
2. There gen-'rous fruits that nev-er fail On trees im-mor-tal grow; There

Ca-naan's fair and hap-py land, Where my pos-ses-sions lie.
rocks and hills and brooks and vales With milk and hon-ey flow.

CHORUS

I am bound for the Prom-ised Land, Bound for the Prom-ised Land. Oh,

who will come and go with me? I am bound for the Prom-ised Land.

3. Oh, the transporting rapt'rous scene
   That rises to my sight:
   Sweet fields arrayed in living green
   And rivers of delight. [Chorus]

4. When shall I reach that happy place
   And be forever blessed?
   When shall I see my Father's face
   And in His bosom rest? [Chorus]

(1866-1899)

5
NEW BEGINNINGS
(1866-1899)

For immigrants and blacks, new freedoms spelled new beginnings. For the country at large, unprecedented economic expansion was to give birth to modern America. With cattle, coal, oil, and steel, giant farms, factories, and railroads, fortunes pyramided into empires that were to push the United States toward the pinnacle of world power. But just as the age of the cowboy came and went, so went the inalienable rights of many. Dashed were the high hopes of blacks now trapped in another form of slavery and those of immigrants in a new form of misery. For some then, an era of new beginnings was to end in broken dreams, their bodies building the land, their souls laid bare in song. The jubilance of "Joshua Fit de Battle of Jericho" was to give way to "Nobody Knows the Trouble I've Seen" and "Drill, Ye Tarriers, Drill," the railroad workers' complaint. Lumberjacks sang about "The Jam on Gerry's Rock"; miners, "My Sweetheart's the Mule in the Mines." Robber barons were put down by "Jay Gould's Daughter," folk heroes set up by "John Henry," and cowboys turned into superheroes as they loped to "I Ride an Old Paint" on "The Old Chisholm Trail."

The postwar state of the union was like a sprawling, brawling young giant in clumsy command of its limbs. The victorious, rapacious North was out to punish a ruined South. In the Middle West, more than wind whistled through the plains as homesteader fought ranger. And in the Far West, the land smeared with Indian massacre, was a violent mix of raw pioneering and wild prosperity.

Lincoln martyred, Andrew Johnson took over the presidency; the South was a ravaged wasteland; its attempts at reconciliation met only by rebuffs. Black Codes (the planter's answer to the Thirteenth Amendment) spelled out a new form of slavery by restricting freedmen to domestic service or farming; exceptions made for prohibitive fees. But the South got its comeuppance the year radical Republicans gained control of Congress. In fast succession they established the Freedmen's Bureau and passed the Civil Rights Act (to be declared unconstitutional in 1883), the Reconstruction Act enforcing civil rights by military occupation, the Fourteenth Amendment granting citizenship to former slaves. The other side of the coin saw profiteering "carpetbaggers" (northern politicians) and "scalawags" (southern conservatives) taking over state governments by means more extralegal than legal. Shocks of terror were to spread through the land with wholesale murder spattering the landscape, the work of Ku Klux Klansmen and Knights of the White Camelia. Yet congressional moves to curb the ghostly riders only drove them underground. Another congressional move doomed to failure was the impeachment (for reasons political, not moral) of President Johnson, who won acquittal by a single vote. By the end of his term in 1869 the Atlantic Cable had been laid, Nebraska made a member of the union, and Alaska bought from Russia for $7,200,000 (less than 2¢ an acre).

At first considered a folly, the purchase proved a bargain—lumber, mining, fishing, trapping, even oil—and a century later, the concern of conservationists. John Muir, one of the earliest conservationists, was to walk one thousand miles from Wisconsin to the Gulf of Mexico, his personal campaign to have Yosemite made a national park. Meanwhile, Wisconsin printer Christopher Sholes was to patent a writing machine he called the typewriter and sell his rights some years later to Remington Arms. Back east the first "el" ran over New York, and, with circuses popular everywhere, "The Man on the Flying Trapeze" the song of the day.

Equally *un*popular was Darwinism, condemned in every church on Sunday, yet acted out by many people on Monday. Only progressive preachers like

Henry Ward Beecher or Phillip Brooks seemed able to reconcile evolution and religion. While church attendance was still compulsory in Vermont and South Carolina, Christian Science was being evolved by Mary Baker Eddy. Boston saw the founding of the YWCA, Nashville, the founding of Fisk University for black women. While some women gingerly tried out curling tongs (ringlets were all the rage), straight-haired Susan B. Anthony was to start *The Revolutionary*, a suffragette paper with the motto "The true republic—men, their rights and nothing more; women, their rights and nothing less." Wyoming agreed and in 1869 (predating the Nineteenth Amendment by fifty-one years) gave women the vote.

In neighboring Utah two locomotives touched noses at Promontary Point and the transcontinental railroad became a reality. The Union Pacific had taken three years and twenty thousand men to build across 1,775 miles of mountains and plains. Before long, steel horses were to pull William Davis's refrigerator cars and George Pullman's dining cars, safely slowing down with the Westinghouse air brake. "They got sidetracked" and "got up a full head of steam" entered the language. "That's a heck of a way to run a railroad" summed up the reaction of most to the many scandals of the day: C. P. Huntington's buying off the California legislature to promote his rail interests; the shenanigans of Cornelius Vanderbilt watering New York Central stock; likewise Gould, Fisk, and Drew the Erie, with disastrous results; the stock market's "Black Friday."

An even blacker day was the one that buried more than one hundred Pennsylvania miners and boy helpers in the Avondale mine disaster. And man-made disasters were crashing all around the country's new leader. Although not personally involved, Ulysses S. Grant was to spend most of his presidency adrift in a sea of corruption. As fraud turned up in the Indian Bureau and Customs Department (speeding the adoption of the Civil Service Act), Tammany boss Tweed and friends ran off with a cool $200 million in New York.

By the opening of the 1870s there were 38.5 million people; a new amendment, the fifteenth, giving everyone (except women) the right to vote; and, returning civil rights to most, the Amnesty Act. Brigham Young was arrested for polygamy; hoops gave way to bustles; linoleum, oleomargarine, and root beer were novelties; the roller-skating craze had spread through the country, and the Chicago fire through six counties, destroying two thousand acres, over one thousand lives.

Fiery women were on the march again. Susan Anthony was indicted for illegal voting, Frances Willard formed the Women's Christian Temperance Union, and another bar dropped as Belva Lockwood became the nation's first woman lawyer. The trade union movement began to attract women. The People's Party chose a woman, Victoria Woodhull, to run for president. When everyone was after the "fast buck" (when weren't they?) a grass-roots coalition of farmers and workers started the National Greenback Party to circulate more money to more Americans. But in an era of scramble and gamble, misfortune struck; the Panic of '73 resulting from overspeculation, overly rapid agricultural growth, worldwide price drops.

A drop in bread prices and rise in quality was to stem from the roller process of making flour. Mechanical refrigeration was to revolutionize meat packing, enabling Armour and Swift to make fortunes. New chemical knowledge changed the brewing of beer, new refining techniques the potential of petroleum. G. B. Selden engineered the internal combustion engine, Stephen Field electrified the "third" rail, cable streetcars took to the hills of San Francisco, and the first steel arch bridge spanned the Mississippi. Edison invented the incandescent light bulb, the "talking machine" (phonograph), and the electric pen, a duplicating device. Another device by another genius, Bell's telephone, would hear people calling "Hello, central" and see the first switchboard installed in the White House for Rutherford B. Hayes. The lines may have been buzzing, but so was the patent office. McGaffey received rights for the vacuum cleaner, the Hyatts for Celluloid, and Glidden for barbed wire—fencing food in and cattle out would make way for bumper crops.

As western folks sang "Home on the Range" a thirty-eighth star (for Colorado) was sewn on the flag. Back east, folks cheered Etta Morgan and her saxophone, danced to "The Atlantic Cable Polka," roared at the antics of Harrigan and Hart. And everywhere, everyone read books—some trashy, some romantic, Horatio Alger's rags-to-riches most of all. Young

people identified with Louisa May Alcott's *Little Men* and *Little Women*, Mark Twain's *Adventures of Tom Sawyer*, Bret Harte's Wild West stories, those in dialect by Indiana's James Whitcomb Riley and Georgia's Joel Chandler Harris. Just as more Americans read books, more and more took to outdoor sports. Hockey came to Boston, tennis to Staten Island, track to colleges and to Churchill Downs the first Kentucky Derby in 1875.

An event the following year involving horses was to come to a tragic end at Little Big Horn when Custer's "Last Stand" claimed the lives of some two hundred cavalrymen. In dramatic contrast, the withdrawal of federal troops from the South, the restoration of home rule, was a cause for joy. Cause for celebration was America's one hundredth birthday—the centennial centering around the republic's cornerstone—Philadelphia. The theme, power; the industrial direction of the United States, unmistakable—machinery far outdistanced agriculture—at the grandest fair the world had ever seen. The more than eight million people passing through its gates (admission 50¢) used every available means to get there, converted freight cars included.

Without so much as a breath, the country went from the great fair to the great rail strike of 1877; two-thirds of the system stopped, millions lost in property damage, and fifty-seven died once federal troops entered Maryland, West Virginia, Pennsylvania, Illinois, and Missouri. The decade's end witnessed the beginning of large-scale unrest in factory, field, and mine, the beginning of colonialism with a naval base on Pago Pago, and the beginning of dime-store retailing the day Woolworth opened his first five-and-ten in Utica, New York.

By the 1880s the variety store had become an American institution, the stock so varied the world called the United States "The Home of Invention" (over twenty-five thousand patents annually). Many

so-called modern conveniences began to appear. Inside the house, men started using safety razors (clean-shaven faces were back in style); women, irons and sewing machines, now electrified. Come summer, everyone blessed the electric fan. Outside, the house shone with standardized paint, something new from Sherwin-Williams. And while snowy streets were being cleared in St. Paul by the first electric plow, people shrieked and horses shied in Boston as Philip Pratt drove by in his electric automobile. Down in Richmond the electric trolley system took folks all over town—stopovers a must at soda fountains for the newest treat, a malted—or to the outskirts with picnic hampers and Eastman's box cameras in hand. Out in Wisconsin, a hydroelectric plant hummed and in Indiana's Wabash, nights were bright with electric light. With I-beams produced by Jones & Laughlin, Louis Sullivan built the nation's first skyscraper, a ten-story building in Chicago, with an Otis elevator rising slowly to the top. And high above New York's East River, Roebling's Brooklyn Bridge was opened to pedestrian and vehicular traffic.

Out of a highly technical age, modern America emerged, its phenomenal profits giving birth to that economic steamroller the "trust," brainchild of Standard Oil's S. C. T. Dodd. But this age also had its richly sentimental side: the air filled with serenades —"Just a Song at Twilight" and "Good Night, Ladies" —on Valentine's Day, letterboxes filled with the laciest, gooiest cards (5¢ to $3) addressed in a florid hand with Waterman's fountain pen. Ladies perfumed

with rose water were to faint less from sentiment than from steel corsets, squeezing, implacably, the ideal eighteen-inch waist. On formal occasions gentlemen callers began to appear in something called the tux, introduced by some swell in Tuxedo Park. Courting now took place in the cluttered parlor, a duster's nightmare, lined with patterned wallpaper and littered with Japanese fans, etchings, family portraits, memorabilia unlimited. Marble-topped tables and chests were heavy, overstuffed chairs and couches hard, with well-turned legs, the pride of manufacturers using the mechanical lathe.

Mechanical advances had been great, but not so the laborer's lot—his only defense the work stoppage, sometimes as many as a thousand a year. The eight-hour day was the crusade, climaxed by the Chicago

Haymarket Bombing of 1886. By some miracle, seventeen thousand Illinois workers—mostly in the building trades—achieved their goal that very year, the year the American Federation of Labor and United Mine Workers came into being. Although working conditions improved somewhat, the average industrial worker still struggled to make ends meet.

At this point, churches, interested in maintaining their parishes, entered the labor picture. Preaching the social gospel—labor's right to organize and strike —they opened their doors for more than Sunday services. They established gyms, clubs, classes, lecture series, and libraries. The Salvation Army opened soup kitchens, lodging houses, and employment bureaus. The nonsectarian approach saw the beginnings of settlement houses, with Jane Addams's Hull House spearheading the way. Many benefiting from their services were immigrants who, on their way into the country, had recently passed the newly installed Statue of Liberty. How ironic that this would be the time the Dawes Act made citizens of the first Americans, the American Indians! Undoubtedly, Helen Hunt Jackson's outrage in *A Century of Dishonor* had made some impression.  Another woman sympathetic to the downtrodden was pioneer photographer Alice Austen who trained her lens on immigrants in the streets and in the slums. But her pictures were never to appear in the new ladies' magazines of the day, *Good Housekeeping* and *The Ladies Home Journal*, a time when "Rockabye Baby" first lulled little infants to sleep.

Singing of quite another order could be heard at the new Metropolitan Opera House, where the glitter of Mrs. Astor's "400" studded the golden horse shoe. After theater it was on to Tony Pastor's for late supper and the latest song hits. Except the night when the only sound was that of falling snow—the blizzard of '88. Snows of like proportions, common in Minnesota and Wisconsin, saw Norwegian settlers putting on skis and skiing become an American sport. Soon golf crossed the ocean from Scotland, while bicycling, an eastern craze, sped west to prairie towns about the time Kansas went dry with Prohibition. The decade faded with the opening of Oklahoma to homesteaders, the fifth tenant moving into the White House within ten years, the conversion of four territories into states, the demise of the cowboy, the rise of the hobo.

The seeds of hoboism had taken root during the Civil War when great numbers of men became ena-

mored of camp life. Dislocated by the war, many found settling back into quiet living impossible and took to wandering. With the lack of trespass laws on railroad property, trainmen made no effort to expell tramps, who found a comfortable home in the boxcar and rode the rails. By the 1890's the hobo, once tolerated as an unavoidable nuisance, had become a liability as pilferage and damage mounted; the swing of a policeman's club turning him fugitive. Actually, the hobo was the least of the railroaders' problems. Fierce competition, overexpansion, and reckless management had driven countless lines right into private banking houses—J. P. Morgan's for one.

But then business failures were widespread in the nineties and rural America had become a billion-dollar debt; the majority of homesteaders had sold out or quit. Undefeated, the farmer was to channel his doubt and distress into the People's Party; its members, known as Populists, supported the most socially advanced platform in United States history. The time was ripe. The Populist whirlwind blew Republicans right out of office.

Radicalism was on the move. The Socialist Labor Party became a political base for masses of workers, mostly immigrants. Within two decades 6.3 million foreigners, lured by the dream of gold in the streets, had crossed the Atlantic. Few would realize the dream; most joined the ranks of the urban poor, their misery documented by Jacob Riis in *How the Other Half Lives*.

Casting a long shadow over sweatshop and slum was the country's latest engineering feat, the twenty-six-story home of Pulitzer's *New York World*. This paper put smiles into Sunday with the first color comics and a running cliff-hanger into the rest of the week—breathless installments filed by Nelly Bly, the delight of readers as she circled the globe in the footsteps of Jules Verne's Phileas Fogg. Another pioneering journalist staked her claim in that valley of tears called advice to the lovelorn—"Dear Dorothy Dix."

But no advice yet invented could cope with the natural catastrophes of 1892: the Atlantic states' heat wave, the California earthquake, and the Pennsylvania oilfields ignited by thunderbolt. Lightning (man-made) struck again in Pennsylvania when steel workers on the Homestead Strike were beaten up by Pinkerton men. Up in Massachusetts violence rocked the town of Fall River the day Lizzie Borden allegedly axed her parents with forty-odd whacks. "Actions speak louder than words," they said, but the reverse was true in the cases of Lizzie and Emma (Goldman). Lizzie never went to jail, but anarchist Emma did; her "new ideas," Marxism and free love, offended yet titillated Americans. Fannie Farmer was to titillate tastes in another way with her *Boston Cooking-School Cookbook* and those with poetic tastes relished the verbal mosaics of Emily Dickinson, departed this world years before publication. But the "Gibson girl" was very much alive, more admired than scorned, although some said, "Niggardly waists and niggardly brains go together." In vogue too were mannish styles: tailored suits, shirtwaists, even divided skirts for bicycling—a hint of freer days ahead. So, while some women loosened their corsets, others tightened them, as the bustle went out and the hour-glass look came in. They may have walked like kangaroos, but ladies held their heads like swans as they balanced those crazy big hats. Dignified, not crazy, was the word for male head coverings, particularly the homburg, a match for the elegance of spats over high button shoes. To fasten his shoes while seated, one Whitcomb Judson, a portly gent, was pressed to invent the first slide fastener. Yet zippers first appeared not on clothes but mail bags, as postmen astride horses, then bikes, rode the first RFD routes.

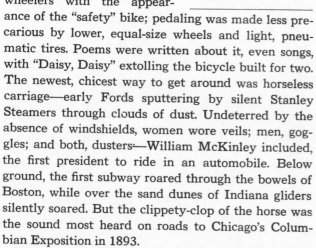

Gone were the old high wheelers with the appearance of the "safety" bike; pedaling was made less precarious by lower, equal-size wheels and light, pneumatic tires. Poems were written about it, even songs, with "Daisy, Daisy" extolling the bicycle built for two. The newest, chicest way to get around was horseless carriage—early Fords sputtering by silent Stanley Steamers through clouds of dust. Undeterred by the absence of windshields, women wore veils; men, goggles; and both, dusters—William McKinley included, the first president to ride in an automobile. Below ground, the first subway roared through the bowels of Boston, while over the sand dunes of Indiana gliders silently soared. But the clippety-clop of the horse was the sound most heard on roads to Chicago's Columbian Exposition in 1893.

The fair's symbol, seen for miles around and some twenty stories high, enough to make heads spin, was the great ferris wheel. On the midway, the Egyptian Village with Little Egypt baring her midriff in a "hootchy-kootchy" dance pulled in males like a light bulb moths. Amusements aside, the largest crowds would ooh and aah as they filed past the wonders in Machinery Hall. But the greatest testament to American technology was the fair site itself—Chicago, risen from the ashes of twenty years before.

The exposition was still running when the country fell into another depression to the shrill accompaniment of industrial strife, crescendoing to a screech with the Pullman Strike of '94. Simultaneous announcements of the usual 8 percent dividend ($2.5 million) and a 25 percent wage cut signaled the beginning of class warfare. President Cleveland, always passive in the face of big business, suddenly sprang into action, smashing the strike with troops and jailing union head Eugene Debs. Restraint of a completely different type was the harnassing of Niagara Falls with the Westinghouse generator, distributing current far and wide. Another powerful giant was the steam hammer, a tool so precise it could rest lightly on an egg or strike heavy blows equaling one hundred and twenty-five tons.

Some little things also came along. On Edison's kinetoscope, prototype of movie camera and projector, features first flickered in penny arcades; the latest diversion at home, the player piano, turning amateur pianists into parlor virtuosi. But, it took some skill to pop a ball into peach baskets hung at opposite ends of a gym by James Naismith, the father of basketball. Taking on a fatherly role was a player of baseball, not basketball, who switched from sports to religion—evangelist Billy Sunday. Riding a different circuit (a good eighteen thousand miles) was presidential hopeful William Jennings Bryan, who delivered his "Cross of Gold" speech the year veins burst with gold in Alaska (1896). Americans (gold-crazy again) rushed to the Klondike, where some struck it rich; Sweetwater Bill Gates, for one, gallantly gave his sweetheart her weight in gold.

But more valuable than gold in 1898 were the country's territorial gains with the annexation of Hawaii, the spoils of the Spanish-American War. After only 114 days of actual combat Spain was to hand over Cuba as a protectorate, cede Puerto Rico, the Phillipines, Guam, and the Sulu Islands, all for a total of twenty million dollars. In little more than a century, the United States had evolved from colonial possession to colonial power.

Inside the country, states now numbered forty-five; the Indian Wars were concluded and Indians confined to reservations; of close to seventy-six million people, one in ten bought newspapers. The climate of democracy had changed, violent contrasts abounded in the land: splendor alongside squalor; sooty nine-year-old slate pickers, velvet-suited fauntleroys; marble "cottages" in Newport, rotting slums in Jersey City; faint idealism and religious fervor; illiterate masses and massive free education; yellow journalism, dogged muckraking; giant corporations dwarfing individuals;

man against machine; city and factory increasing, farm and village decreasing; geographical distances shrinking, population disparity growing; Sherman Anti-Trust braking monopoly, labor legislation monitoring industry—the slow death of laissez faire, the painful birth of social reform; the conditions across the continent, the cross-section of people, more varied, more extreme than ever before.

In the North, with machinery and industry supreme, older methods of carrying on business radically changed. Compared to the bustle of cities, rural life remained relatively calm, with minimal changes in farm life between the Civil War and the coming of the car. Folks rose early, worked late, rested little. The core of family living in frame houses was still the kitchen; the parlor used only for courting, funerals, and weddings. Under the reflected glow of a kerosene lamp the stereopticon shared the marbletop table with a Rogers plaster sculpture—*Fetching the Doctor* or *Weighing the Baby*; for the more affluent, a Tiffany vase on the table, an Eakins or a Homer on the wall, an iron deer on the lawn. In drafty houses (rheumatism cured with skunk oil) hands were warmed over the fire or cast-iron stove; gas came later. Fewer than 10 percent of American farmhouses before 1900 had plumbing; the weekly bath was still taken in the wooden washtub.

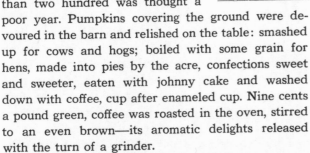

Crocks of off-white butter, without carrot juice to turn it gold, were stored in the cellar. The woods were picked clean of berries to put up in jars for winter; less than two hundred was thought a poor year. Pumpkins covering the ground were devoured in the barn and relished on the table: smashed up for cows and hogs; boiled with some grain for hens, made into pies by the acre, confections sweet and sweeter, eaten with johnny cake and washed down with coffee, cup after enameled cup. Nine cents a pound green, coffee was roasted in the oven, stirred to an even brown—its aromatic delights released with the turn of a grinder.

Outside, the addition of a porch allowed for the spreading of work and play. The hired hand, a part of the family, dressed up on Saturday and drove his horse and buggy to town for some fun. At the barbershop, center for sporting intelligence and smut, waiting customers puffed the new cigarettes or broke out in "barbershop chords." Down the street the feed store

and general emporium, a new school, two or three churches, shingles for a lawyer and doctor (who turned dentist and vet on occasion), and possibly an "opera house" made up the town.

At night, serenading parties were great fun. At ten o'clock, after a hearty supper, instruments tuned in the parlor and trial duets with much giggling, off they went in the hay wagon, dangling lanterns behind.

Although there was precious little serenading in the South, music helped Southerners forget their defeat, their continuing burdens during Reconstruction. Many a household and community found solace around the organ or piano. With over two billion dollars in slave property wiped out, no seed for planting, no currency, four million blacks waited for "forty acres and a mule." Carpetbaggers owning most southern stomachs and souls saw the start of sharecropping, tenant farming, the virgin tapping of coal and iron resources. The Old South was just a memory in the imagination of poets, novelists, and playwrights.

In queen cities like Charleston, fancy restaurants and fabulous homes, ironwork rusting, were boarded up in silence within splendid gardens. Outside ragged hedges, animated street life resumed. New ingredients: soldiers, Union and Confederate, up-country refugees, plantation blacks, creating a restless raucousness day and night punctuated by the happy sound of organ grinders.

Towns were sliced into sections: downtown, business; around town, residential; along tracks and riversides, in essence the leavings, the homes of blacks. Twice a week all mingled on market day. Always passing through were traveling ventriloquists, circuses, and, for the more socially exclusive, tournaments in medieval costume acting out Sir Walter Scott. Popular too, were horseracing, state fairs, Mardi Gras carnivals, and the newest fad, baseball, with clubs calling themselves "Up and At 'Em," "Up and Skunk 'Em." But free public hangings beat them all, with blacks turning them into grand jubilees.

As the breakup of plantations emptied slave quarters, former slaves were to resettle in cabins clustered around the church, the cotton gin, and the general store—a novel delight as well as lifeline to the outside world. Social life, what there was of it, radiated from the church, its whitewashed walls garlanded with paper flowers and, after dark, resounding with powerful song.

Mountain families singing hymns might be joined by the musical howls of hounds after a supper often shared with a traveler—hot corn cake from the open fire, wild honey, and milk. On his way out at dawn, past the spinning wheel on the porch, the guest was soon lost in the haze; left behind, the lonely cabin, the hidden valley, the mountaineer's isolation, a life of little talk and much work to eke out crops of corn and wheat.

Rural life was wrenched out of its socket in mountain and wood, hill and coastal plain, the transformation painful. Life had drastically changed for many. The majority made for the nearest large town or city, with poor whites migrating in droves to Texas. Alone or in groups, blacks set out to discover what freedom meant; Georgia lost twenty thousand to the West one year.

Within two decades nine million immigrants crossed the Mississippi, settling the prairie and points west. Armed with new freedom and the pioneering spirit, they weathered the perils of dust storms, floods, blizzards, grass fires, droughts, hot winds, even grasshopper plagues. Not only immigrants trekked west, but itinerants: rainmakers, lightning rod swindlers, and medicine showmen—Diamond Dick one of the most famous. The medicine show, a well-trained troupe skilled at scaring up crowds and entertaining, was expert at creating a frenzied climate for the pitchman.

The medicine show was only passing through, but with its share of snake oil ads, the pioneer newspaper was there before the post office, the jail, the school or the church, and, of course, the saloon. A fixture of all frontier towns, the saloon in farm communities was peaceful, compared to cow and mining towns, where levity and intemperance was a relief from long seasons of privation and hardship. The tough atmosphere of the saloon produced some pretty tough, yet colorful characters. Both sides of the law came swinging through doors in the personages of Wyatt Earp, Bat Masterson, Billy the Kid and Wild Bill Hickock, the Daltons and the Jameses. Women too, were a part of the scene, decorating tables or feet on the rail: Annie Oakley, Calamity Jane, and Belle Starr. In the back room, billiards; outside in the dirt lot, baseball; on the green, bowling or croquet—a courting game with no equal in the new West.

And everywhere, at the drop of whatever, there was dancing, dancing, dancing—the most sought-after partner swinging his lady, to kick the ceiling, swinging and kicking again, keeping perfect time to the music. Cheers were loud and long, especially on the Fourth of July, when catching the greased pig, climbing the greased pole, racing in tubs on the river, or riding the homemade merry-go-round pulled by horse or mule added joy.

But the next day, the horse not pulling a merry-go-round reminded everybody that the real ruler of the prairie was the cattle rancher. Beyond his barbed-wire boundaries loomed the freedom of the richly forested Far West, the last frontier where man answered only to the elements. Out of nature's riches evolved a spartan life: the log house put together with pegs; fire in the hearth, like an eternal flame, for heating and cooking; the big black iron pot filled with everything from beans to bread; sparse furnishings, stout and raw; the trunk and quilt, treasures from the past. Treasured too was the single glass window, required by law to hold one's claim, passed from neighbor to neighbor with sheep hide nailed back after the inspector's visit.

Pioneers took chances with nothing, planting their crops by the phases of the moon: top crops—peas, beans, squash—under waxing moons; root crops—carrots, potatoes, turnips—under waning moons. But come Saturday night, caution thrown to the winds, carefree merriment was the rule. By nine the house was aglow with guests, children included. Everyone danced like fools, stopping only to mop faces, caller replacing caller. From the moment the fiddler raised his bow, floor boards shook, stopping just once before dawn. At midnight came the smell of food; folks simmered down and turned to tables laden with prize recipes from grouse and pheasant to bear and deer meat; salmon, trout, and smelts, smoked and fresh; vegetables cooked in sugary syrup with ginger, green-tomato mince pie; the favorite and simplest dessert, vinegar pie topped with meringue—all washed down with whiskey, cider, or milk. Somehow, youngsters always managed to wake up for supper, tumbling out of makeshift beds to return as refueled grown-ups danced faster and faster. At sun-up, weary but happy, all put away a hearty breakfast of eggs, hot cakes, side pork, and coffee. Stomachs full, legs tired, voices hoarse, they took their leave till another Saturday, another house, brought them together again.

Out in the blustery Northwest, the lumberjack left rich deposits in the treasury of American folk song. In the pits of Pennsylvania and Kentucky it was the miner. Railroaders laying track, the strongest voices Irish, were an international mix. Cowboys, saddlebags filled with song, crossed paths with vocal prairie farmers. Wherever the search for freedom took them, spirituals went with blacks. Even the hobo, free and in search of nothing in particular, contributed his share. One thing they all had in common was dreams. And whatever happened to be on their minds as they broke their backs seemed to find expression in song. Rhythms and types of work were strong inspirations; the focuses, danger, escape, humor, hardship, and man versus machine—as in the epic ballad "John Henry," pounding out the rhythm of the hammer, one man's battle against the steam drill. Another black song set to a different beat was "Pick a Bale of Cotton"; the workers' singing, the loudest sound in the field, a stunning contrast to the blasting of roadbed so humorously put in "Drill, Ye Tarriers, Drill!" This was only one of many songs contributed by Irish workmen as they pick-and-shoveled their way across a continent alongside other immigrants, Chinese included. Some of the earliest Chinese immigrants took to surface mining, for some reason or other reluctant to go underground, unlike the Welsh and Polish in the Appalachians.

With singing impossible while working below ground, miners' songs, developed out of protest, were songs of leisure. They reflected the fears, hopes, hardships, and mishaps of the profession: "The Mines of Avondale," "The Shoofly," "Down, Down, Down," and the comic exception, "My Sweetheart's the Mule in the Mines." Mule drivers, often as young as fourteen—having started perhaps at eight as slate pickers, graduating to doorkeepers at ten—learned their history and geography at night in the singing of songs, verses improvised by the schoolmaster in a one-room "patch" school. With each mine "patch" developing its own minstrelsy, the school eventually became the singing school.

The soot on the hobo's face came from coal all right, but not from hard work. He could afford to have his nonsense songs—"It Was Midnight on the Ocean"—or to express his fantasies with style—"Big Rock Candy Mountain"—or as his train rolled through the prairie to sing "The Ninety and Nine."

The wheat-producing prairie would provide a passel of songs; "The Farmer Is the Man," the most representative, singing his worth, bolstering his ego through hard times.

Hard times and the hard life of the cowboy: the sky his roof for weeks at a time, his clothes unchanged, the monotony of beans and coffee, his only companions the animals he rode and drove. How odd that such a dry life should yield such richness— trail songs, lullabies, taming songs, laments, and legends: "Sam Bass," "Red River Valley," "The Horse Wrangler," "The Cowboy's Lament," and "Dodgin' Joe," a black cowboy song. (One in eight was black.) By the 1890s moving cattle long distances was the job of railroads; black former cowboys joined the competition as Pullman porters—one of the risks, an occasional robbery by Jesse James (lionized in song).

Lumberjacks, sturdy individualists like cowboys, gloried in their prowess, as illustrated by the legend of Paul Bunyan. The hazards and somber tragedies of their calling supplied ample themes for their ballads starting with "The Lumberman's Alphabet"—"D is for danger, we often fall in"—leading up to the tragic accidents of "James Whaland" and "The Jam on Gerry's Rock." Romance also had a place in shantymen's hearts, with "Shanty Boy and Shanty Girl" and "The Little Eau Pleine." After the evening meal or on Sunday, the bunk shanty echoed with song to the accompaniment of mouth organ or jaw's harp, and on Saturday night, stag dances.

Though trips to town were rare, lumberjacks might catch a show at the local "opera house." Traveling troupes seemed to have a knack for smelling out the newest towns where people applauded everything from the clanging of a family of Swiss bell ringers to a sublime solo by Fritz Kreisler to entertainments by black performers Jim Crow Rice or Blind Sam and His Brothers.

This could be called the era of America's musical awakening. Patrick Gilmore, the Barnum of the band business (credited with "When Johnny Comes Marching Home") put on mammoth shows in Boston, unprecedented in size, unparalleled in vulgarity. With a baton six feet long he conducted an orchestra of a thousand musicians, forty soloists, and a mixed chorus of ten thousand, with cannons roaring, churchbells pealing, even fifty firemen beating out the "Anvil Chorus"! No match for all that, certainly, but a star in his own right, was more restrained John Philip Sousa, composer of "Stars and Stripes Forever." Less flamboyant and slower to start were chamber groups and symphony orchestras—towering leaders of the day Theodore Thomas and Leopold Damrosch introducing American composers MacDowell, Chadwick,

Foote, and Mrs. Beach. Among those who worked in a lighter vein was Reginald DeKoven, his operetta *Robin Hood* is long forgotten, but one of its songs still

moistens the eye of many a wedding guest—the enduring "O Promise Me."

Musical thirsts were freshly slaked with opera and concert series, periodicals and books, and music teaching was finally recognized as a profession. States added music to the curriculums of public schools; the federal government, a music division to the Library of Congress.

The music released from new institutions was also to come from those breaking up. From the plantation, hot Afro-American folk music combined with black plantation culture—coon songs and cakewalk dances done to the pick and strum of a banjo. After the Civil War, black music and dance left the plantations and strutted happily onto minstrel stages. In cities and towns black brass bands blaring hot rhythms began to rag marches into ragtime. From plucking banjos to blowing brass to hammered strings (the piano), ragtime was perfected in the bawdy house by honky-tonk players, and Scott Joplin was king of them all—his "Maple Leaf Rag" a hit in 1899.

But more respectable in those days were the touring Fisk Jubilee Singers. Audiences black and white in hamlet and town, more often than not, left the concert hall humming "Gospel Train," "Swing Low, Sweet Chariot," "Deep River," and "My Lord, What a Morning!"

Nobody Knows the Trouble I've Seen

Traditional

Solemnly

mp No-bod-y knows the trou-ble I've seen. No-bod-y knows but Je-sus.

No-bod-y knows the trou-ble I've seen, Glo-ry, hal-le-lu-jah! *Fine*

1. One morn-ing I was a-walk-ing 'round,— Oh, yes, Lord! I
2. I pick the berry and I suck the juice, — Oh, yes, Lord! It's
3. Some-times I'm up, some-times I'm down, _ Oh, yes, Lord! Some-

Last time D.C. al fine

saw some ber-ries a-hang-ing down, _ Oh, yes, Lord!
just as sweet as the hon-ey-comb, _ Oh, yes, Lord!
times I'm al-most on the groun', _ Oh, yes, Lord!

John Henry

Traditional

Steady boogie

1. John Henry was a little baby,
Sittin' on his gran'ma's knee;
Oh, he lift up a hammer and a little chunk of steel,
Said, "This hammer's gonna be the death of me. Lord, Lord. Yes, this hammer's gonna be the death of me."

2. The captain says to John Henry,
"Gonna bring a steel drill 'round,
Gonna take that drill out on the road,
Gonna drive that steel on down. Lord, Lord. Gonna drive that steel on down."

3. John Henry drove through fourteen feet,
The steam drill only drove nine;
But he drove so hard that he broke his poor heart,
And he laid down his hammer and he died. Lord, Lord.
Yes, he laid down his hammer and he died.

4. They took John Henry to the graveyard
And they buried him deep in sand.
Now ev'ry train that comes a-chuggin' round
Says, "Here lies a steel-drivin' man." Lord, Lord.
Says, "Here lies a steel-drivin' man."

Drill, Ye Tarriers, Drill!

Energetically

Traditional

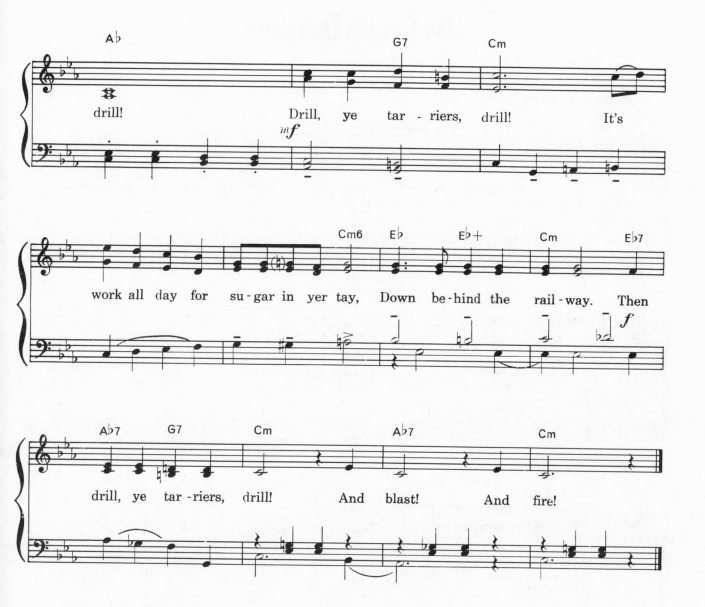

3. Now the foreman's name was Jim McGann.
   By gosh, he was a blame mean man.
   Last week a premature blast went off;
   A mile in the air went big John Goff. [*Chorus*]

4. When next payday came around,
   John Goff a dollar short was found.
   So he asked, "What for?" Came this reply:
   "Yer docked for the time you were in the sky." [*Chorus*]

Jay Gould's Daughter

Traditional

Rollin' along

1. On a Mon-day morn-ing it be-gan to rain. A - round the bend came a
2. Jay Gould's daugh-ter said be-fore she died, "There's one more road that I'd

pas - sen - ger train. On the bump-ers was a ho-bo John, He's a
like __ to ride." "Tell me, daugh-ter, what __ can it be?" "It's in

good old ho - bo, but he's dead and gone. Dead and gone, __
west - ern Tex - as on the San - ta Fe. San - ta Fe, __

dead and gone; __ A good old ho - bo, but he's dead and gone.
San - ta Fe; __ In west-ern Tex - as on the San - ta Fe.

Big Rock Candy Mountain

Traditional

Fervently

mf

1. One night just as the sun went down And the jun-gle fires were burn-ing,

Down the track comes a bur-ly bum And he said, "Boys I'm not turn-ing. I'm

head-ed for a land that's far a-way Be-side the crys-tal foun-tain; I'll

see you all this com-ing fall In the Big Rock Can-dy Moun-tain." 2. In the

The Little Eau Pleine

Traditional

4. "If Joe Murphy's the name of your raftsman,
   I used to know him quite well.
   But sad is the tale I must tell you:
   Your Joseph was drowned in the Dells;
   They buried him near a scrub Norway;
   You'll never behold him again;
   No stone marks the spot where your raftsman
   Lies far from the Little Eau Pleine."

5. "My curses attend you, Wisconsin!
   May your rapids and falls cease to roar;
   May every towhead and sand bar
   Be as dry as a long schoolhouse floor;
   May the willows upon all your islands
   Lie down like a field of ripe grain,
   For taking my jolly young raftsman
   Away from the Little Eau Pleine."

The Farmer Is the Man

Traditional

1. Oh, the far-mer comes to town With his wag-on bro-ken down. Oh, the far-mer is the man who feeds them all. You need on-ly look and see, And I'm sure you will a-gree That the far-mer is the man who feeds them all. The

far - mer is the man, The far - mer is the man,

Lives on cred - it till the fall; { 1. & 2. Then they take him by the hand And they
3. With the in-terest rate so high It's a

lead him from the land, While the mer-chant is the one who gets it all.
won-der he don't die, For the cred - i - tor's the one who gets it all.

2. Oh, the lawyer hangs around
While the butcher cuts a pound.
    Oh, the farmer is the man who feeds them all.
And the preacher and the cook
Go a-strolling by the brook.
    Oh, the farmer is the man who feeds them all. [*Chorus*]

3. When the banker says he's broke
And the merchant's up in smoke,
    They forget that it's the farmer feeds them all.
It would put them to the test
If the farmer took a rest;
    Then they'd know that it's the farmer feeds them all. [*Chorus 3*]

The Jam on Gerry's Rock

Traditional

1. Come round, you brave young ri-ver-men and list' while I re-
2. It was on a Sun-day morn-ing, in the ear-ly spring one

late The sto-ry of a shan-ty boy and
year. The logs were pil-ing moun-tain-high; no

his un-hap-py fate. The tale con-cerns a
one could keep them clear. "Turn out, turn out, my

man-ly lad, so tall, so true and brave; 'Twas
shan-ty boys, un-load your hearts of woe; We'll

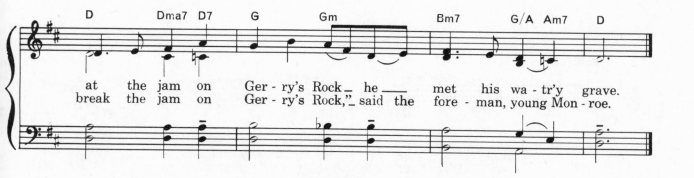

at the jam on Ger - ry's Rock __ he __ met his wa - tr'y grave.
break the jam on Ger - ry's Rock," __ said the fore - man, young Mon - roe.

3. Now, some of them were willing and some hid out of sight,
For breaking jams on Sunday they didn't think was right.
But six of our brave rivermen soon volunteered to go
And break the jam on Gerry's Rock with the foreman, young Monroe.

4. They had not rolled off many logs till their foreman he did say,
"Watch out, young boys, be on your guard, for the jam will soon give way."
But scarce had he spoke the warning, when the jam did break and go.
It carried off those six brave lads with their foreman, young Monroe.

5. And when the rest of the shanty boys the sad news they did hear,
In search of their dead comrades down the river they did steer.
Some of the mangled bodies a-floating on did go,
While smashed and bleeding near the bank was that of young Monroe.

6. They dragged him from that river bank, swept back his raven hair.
A fair maid was among them whose loud cries rent the air:
Claire Clark, she was a noble girl, the riverman's true friend,
Who with her widowed mother lived by the river's bend.

7. They buried him with sorrow deep around the first of May,
And wages of Claire's own true love the boss to her did pay.
Yet soon to her the shanty boys a gift of gold did give,
But with a heart so badly broke she had not long to live.

8. Her last request was granted her: to lie by the dear one's side.
Come, all of you bold rivermen, and pray for him who died.
Engraved upon the hemlock tree that by the grave did grow
Was the name and date and the sad, sad fate of the shanty boy Monroe.

Red River Valley

Traditional

The Old Chisholm Trail

Traditional

3. I'm up in the mornin' before daylight,
   And 'fore I gits to sleepin' the moon's shinin' bright. [*Refrain*]

4. Oh, it's bacon and beans almost ev'ry day,
   And I'd sooner be a-eatin' plain prairie hay. [*Refrain*]

5. I went to the boss for to draw my roll!
   He had it figured I was nine dollars in the hole. [*Refrain*]

6. So I went to the boss and said, "I won't take that,"
   And I slapped him in the face with my old slouch hat. [*Refrain*]

7. I'll sell my outfit just as soon as I can,
   'Cause I ain't punchin' cattle for no mean boss man. [*Refrain*]

8. With my knees in the saddle and my seat in the sky
   I'll quit punchin' cattle in the sweet by and by. [*Refrain*]

Git Along, Little Dogies

Traditional

2. It's early in spring when we round up the dogies.
   We mark 'em and brand 'em and bob off their tails,
   Then round up the horses and load the chuck wagon,
   And throw the little dogies upon the long trail. [*Chorus*]

3. It's whoopin', it's yellin', it's drivin' the dogies.
   Oh, how I wish they would git along!
   It's a-whoopin' and a-punchin' and "Git along, little dogies,
   For you know that Wyoming will be your new home." [*Chorus*]

My Sweetheart's the Mule in the Mines

Traditional Words
Music by *James Thornton*

Down in the Coal Mine

J.B. Geehegan (1872)

With spirit

1. I am a jov-ial col-lier lad, as blithe as blithe can be; For
2. My hands are horn-y, hard, and black with work-ing in the vein, And,

let the times be good or bad, they're all the same to me. 'Tis
like the clothes up - on my back, my speech is rough and plain. Well,

lit-tle of the world I know and care less for its ways, For
if I stum-ble with my tougue, one ex-cuse to say: It's

where the dog star nev-er glows, I wear a-way my days.
not the col-lier's heart that's wrong, 'tis the head that's gone a-stray.

CHORUS

_f_ Down, down in the coal mine, un - der-neath the ground,

Where a gleam of sun - shine nev - er can be found.

Dig - ging dusk - y dia - monds all the year a - round,

Down, down in the coal mine, un - der-neath the ground.

3. How little do the great ones care, who sit at home secure,
   What hidden dangers colliers dare, what hardships they endure.
   The very fires their mansions boast to cheer themselves and wives
   Mayhap were kindled at the cost of jovial colliers' lives. [_Chorus_]

4. Then, cheer up, lads, and make ye much of every joy you can,
   But let your mirth be always such as best becomes a man.
   However Fortune turns about, we'll still be jovial souls.
   What would this country be without the lads that look for coals? [_Chorus_]

When Johnny Comes Marching Home

Traditional

(1900-1929)

6
WORLD POWER
(1900-1929)

It was as though the nation had charged into the twentieth century and never stopped for breath till the '29 crash. In the first twenty years alone the changes were phenomenal: the car, the airplane, World War I, and women's suffrage; radio, moving pictures, and in music, blues ragged into jazz. Played against the shift in focus from country to city, the frenzied industrial drama unfolded with festering fury in field and factory, mill and mine, opening a rich vein of song. The twenties produced still different music, for by then the United States was the world's greatest power, somewhat giddy with prosperity, terror-stricken by Palmer Raids, reeling from Teapot Dome and bathtub gin. Flappers, gangsters, and the "lost generation"; workers, Wobblies, and the dispossessed were to play out the decade in an ever lengthening shadow of doom. How ironic that the most dispossessed and the poorest paid were to contribute the most musical riches to an era paved by Tin Pan Alley. A wealth of song: from "Boll Weevil" and "Midnight Special" to "Pie in the Sky" and "Hinky Dinky Parlay-Voo-Voo!" from "Hard Times in the Mill" and "The Poor Working Girl" to "Frankie and Johnny" and on and on.

By 1900 a strong middle class had emerged as a progressive, humanitarian force. Close to two million child laborers earned little more than two bits daily; newspaper dailies numbered two thousand; pieces of mail annually, over seven billion. The new ILGWU (International Ladies Garment Workers' Union) attacked the thirty-cent daily wage, the seventy-hour week; Casey Jones died at the throttle; the Socialist Party was born. Floradora girls minced across the stage singing "Tell Me, Pretty Maiden"; Gibson girls "In the Good Old Summertime" bared stockinged legs in the surf; bold hussies, their arms a few years later. Tennis saw the first Davis Cup and publishing the first *Smart Set*, a magazine dedicated to the exotic

and the naughty. Carnegie shelled out millions for libraries; Rockefeller, for medical research; and Walter Reed made the connection between mosquito and yellow fever.

When McKinley was struck down by a bullet the "Bully Pulpit" was taken over by irrepressible Teddy Roosevelt, a joy to political cartoonists. Always good copy, the sports-loving champion of the little man spread a wrestling mat for jujitsu, a welcome mat for Booker T. Washington (shocking Southerners) the day he came to lunch. A match for her president, forty-three-year-old Annie Edson Taylor barreled over Niagara Falls; for the less daring, the new mini-sport, Ping Pong; for big spenders like Lillian Russell and Diamond Jim, Jamaica Racetrack; for average Californians, the first Tournament of Roses football game. Muckrakers tackled big business, Ida Tarbell exposed Standard Oil, Lincoln Steffens decried *The Shame of the Cities*, poet Edwin Markham championed "The Man with the Hoe," and Helen Keller's autobiography gave heart to the handicapped. Boston shop girls earned five to six dollars a week, rayon was patented, army uniforms changed from blue to olive drab. *New York Herald* reporter Rosenfeld, with the sound of tinny pianos in his ear, nicknamed music publishers' row Tin Pan Alley. People in Omaha now called relatives in New York, millionaires sang in shower baths, sports fans got hoarse at the first World Series (Boston beat Pittsburgh), *The Great Train Robbery* thrilled picture-show goers. Two bicycle-shop owners, the Wright brothers, built a flying machine and made history in 1903 at Kitty Hawk. Fetch and Krarup, cheered cross-country, drove their Packard from San Francisco to New York (less than two hundred miles paved) in fifty-two days. New York's speed laws: 20 mph in open country, 15 in villages, 10 in town. On Fifth Avenue, a woman was arrested in her auto for smoking; celebrated men were paid for cigarette ads.

"Shirt sleeves," "get rich quick," "kissing bug" were new phrases and topics in the news circa 1904, as were growing divorce, installment buying (notably of diamond rings), stars sparkling in Mt. Wilson's Observatory, and the St. Louis fair, where balloonists received free hydrogen, pianos tinkled "Meet Me in St. Louis," and hungry fairgoers ate the first hot dogs on buns. Sears promised customers its steam-powered washing machine ($5.00) could do the job without them, but feather-crazy women couldn't do without their seventy-five kinds of plumes—the newly formed

National Audubon Society forming a first line of defense for the birds. Conservation-minded Teddy Roosevelt captured the hearts of Americans big and small for the second time; small ones cuddled Teddy bears, big ones read the *Ladies Home Journal* exposé of Mrs. Winslow's Soothing Teething Medicine (spiked with morphine). Eugene Debs established the Wobblies (IWW: International Workers of the World), the first Rotary Club served lunch, Steiglitz's "291" gallery introduced modern art and photography as art, *Variety* (the show business Bible) made its bow. Barefoot Ruth St. Denis in all her veils lifted the curtain on modern dance, Jelly Roll Morton's "King Porter Stomp" embellished jazz, sentimentalists made "I Love You Truly" a hit. TR married off his daughter in an Alice blue gown and let his sailor-suited son go off to public school unattended to join schoolgirls in middy blouses.

The Pure Food and Drug Act (Upton Sinclair's *The Jungle* a catalyst) was the muckraker's harvest the year Frisco quaked. And the economy quaked months later with the Panic of 1907—Veblen's "business cycle" notwithstanding. Punctuating the gloom were the peek-a-boo shirtwaist (a fraternity pin over the heart), the first Ziegfeld Follies, and the forty-sixth state—Oklahoma. In art, the harsh realities of the "ashcan school" exemplified by Sloan countered the elegance of Sargent. In architecture, a towering spiritual force, Frank Lloyd Wright, broke new ground. In sports the physical force of Jack Johnson

made him heavyweight champ, a title he held for eight years, knocking out one "white hope" after another. Another big winner was Ford's Model T, with extras for pumping water, plowing fields, and generating electricity.

President Taft showed versatility in pushing through laws reforming interstate commerce and management of natural resources, revising federal court injunction proceedings, initiating Postal Savings and the National Health Bureau. In 1909 Peary planted the Stars and Stripes on the North Pole, Americans licked ice cream cones, Bud Fisher drew the first "Mutt and Jeff." Bakelite came out of the mold; barbers sold the side part; and fashion, the sunshade, hobble skirt, and kneelength sweater. While "outdoor girl" Eleanora Sears ran the gamut from fullbacking to flying, three thousand suffragettes in yellow sashes strode through Manhattan and the NAACP (National Association for the Advancement of Colored People) marched into court.

1911's Triangle factory fire killing 145 and maiming hundreds more focused attention on unsafe sweatshops and the need for better working conditions. Militant unionist Mary ("Mother") Jones at eighty saw child labor cut in half *off* the farm, school made compulsory in many states. Scholastic innovations: Thorndike tests and Montessori methods (playthings as learning tools) came in just as folks began calling high schools "people's colleges." Edith Wharton's *Ethan Frome* joined *Frank Merriwell at Yale*, grownups and kids loved "Bringing Up Father," "Buster Brown," and "Krazy Kat." Berlin's "Alexander's Ragtime Band" hit its peak, and a menagerie of ragtime dances overtook the two-step: the turkey trot, the kangaroo dip, the snake, the grizzly bear, and the bunny hug. Daring damsels patted noses with cornstarch, young gallants puffed on cigarettes. Advertising (which arrived with the car—a symbol of the good life) made the luxuries of yesterday the necessities of today.

The *Titanic* struck an iceberg and sank (1912); a more powerful IWW emerged (Lawrence, Mass., struck by textile workers). Adding New Mexico and Arizona, the United States totaled forty-eight. Mary Pickford and Lionel Barrymore starred in *The New York Hat*, based on a $15 story by teen-aged Anita Loos. Teen-agers joined the Girl Scouts; women wore wristwatches; men broke fewer arms cranking cars, thanks to Kettering's self-starter; Pittsburgh had the world's first "drive-in" gas station, and pumps soon disappeared from fronts of hardware stores; seventy thousand motorcycles (the jeeps of World War I) roared out of factories.

Americans grumbled about income taxes (the Sixteenth Amendment passed in 1913), and grieved for the victims of mine disasters in New Mexico and floods in Ohio, Indiana, and Texas. Mr. Mennen put shaving cream in a tube. Dr. McCullough identified the first vitamin, and orange juice joined Kellogg's cornflakes at the breakfast table. When summer brought the tango, skirts split, the dance spread, and couples tangoed in the sands at Brighton, in the streets of Denver.

The next year, World War I broke out in Europe; a canal broke through Panama. Wilson's "New Freedoms," a moderate reform program, activated the Federal Trade Commission; aid to farmers, merchant seamen, and labor unions; the Federal Reserve; direct election of senators. Keystone Kop director Sennett shot *Tillie's Punctured Romance* with Marie Dressler and Charlie Chaplin, *Penrod* and *Tarzan* hit the bookstalls, and football kicked off the season at the Yale Bowl—America's first great stadium. Red flannel underwear went out as Sear's "warm air heating plants" ($70) came in. Down $500 from 1908, the "flivver" drove off assembly lines and out of showrooms for $360 (silent-film stars could have bought thirty a week!). Griffith's *Intolerance* would bewilder some, Nevada's "easy-divorce" law release others, Margaret Sanger's birth-control clinic anger many, the incorporation of the Boy Scouts delight all. Child labor decreased, foreign immigration ceased, and, filling the void, black immigration north increased (three hundred thousand recruited by industry in 1916). The demand for labor rose as did salaries, still slim compared to the profits of "war millionaires." Tearooms appeared on Main Street with cleaning, pressing, and shoe repair shops; tea carts were rolled around homes.

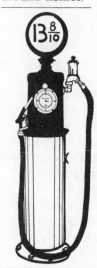

In 1917, America entered the war "to make the world safe for democracy," despite first congresswoman Jeanette Rankin, who cast the sole vote against it, as she would against World War II. Men responded to James Montgomery Flagg's "I Want You" poster, the first American troops went "Over There" with Black Jack Pershing in command. Over here, Langmuir quietly unlocked the secrets of molecular chemistry while the navy enlisted 11,000 yeomen (F), standing for female, and the marine corps 269 women marines (called "marinettes" behind their backs). Pioneer aviator Ruth Law flew over the western front, and "America's Sweetheart," entertained troops in doughboy garb as women turned Western Union messenger, elevator operator, factory laborer, repairshop worker, and "farmerette." The Red Cross got women to roll bandages and knit; blue banners with stars hung in windows; khaki was declared a smart color. Civilians, led by Girl Scouts, collected tons of peach pits to be burned into charcoal for gasmask filters. Boys released from high school (without losing academic credit) helped plant twenty-five million acres of spring wheat within twenty-five days. Despite scarcities, rationing was voluntary. Citizens observed wheatless and heatless Mondays, meatless Tuesdays, grainless Wednesdays, porkless Thursdays and Saturdays, and children were encouraged to eat the whole apple, "patriotic to the core." Ultrapatriotism, liberty bonds, victory gardens flourished; things German submerged: sauerkraut became liberty cabbage; dachshunds, liberty pups; pretzels vanished from saloons.

A coal shortage, in one of the coldest winters, quickly fueled the flu epidemic that snuffed out five hundred thousand lives, four times the number in trenches. All breathed a sigh of relief, some thought it a good omen, when the armistice was signed on the eleventh hour, the eleventh day, the eleventh month of the year 1918. Street bands welcomed troops home with "The Last Long Mile," jazz bands blared "Dardanella." As victory parades petered out, closed cars came in and bars closed up (Prohibition declared by the Eighteenth Amendment). People enjoyed sinful Theda Bara, virtuous Lillian Gish, the naturalism of Anderson's *Winesburg, Ohio.* Seventeen-year-old Bobby Jones cupped the golf crown; heavyweight Jack Dempsey TKO'd Jess Willard, and Congress the same to President Wilson, rejecting both Versailles Treaty and League of Nations—Wilson collapsed, a broken man.

New Year's Day 1920 saw Palmer Raids (against the Red Menace) round up thousands of radicals. A rash of racial and religious intolerance (Ford's *Dearborn Independent* spreading anti-Semitism) broke out in northern cities; riots in Chicago and Tulsa; the South, a trail of charred crosses blazed by KKK. The lovableness of Coogan, "The Kid," was infectious; the rule of baseball's first czar, Judge Landis, firm. Other firsts: women in the polling booth, the League of Women Voters, election returns over Pittsburgh's KDKA. Handsome Harding (silent Coolidge at his side), the choice of bosses in a smoke-filled room, was to be elected on a platform of "Not nostrums, but normalcy"; conservative ex-president Taft, elevated to

Supreme Court chief justice, his ultimate dream.

But a national nightmare was about to begin. With the source bottled up by Prohibition, alcohol went underground to gush forth in the speakeasy ("Charlie sent me"), making the bootlegger the man of the hour. Underworld kingpins Scarface Al Capone, Bugs Moran, and Dutch Shultz masterminded rum-running, hijacking, payoffs, rub-outs—"de woiks." With police corruption near universal, trucks and boats slipped through the law, booze through borders. With the St. Valentine's Day Massacre, gangsterism came to a messy climax in a decade splattered with more than five hundred gangland deaths, half a million arrests, three hundred thousand convictions.

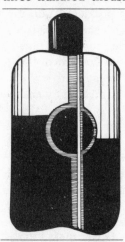

At the edge of the mess in states officially dry stood defiantly wet Rhode Island; never ratifying Prohibition. There, good stuff sold in groceries for $10; elsewhere, enterprising types fermented, distilled, and homebrewed in bathtubs, basements, attics, and backyards.

Officially cutting off the immigration tap, the Johnson Act (1921) established a quota system to weed out "undesirables"; its roots, economic. Man o' War was the horse of the year in a year when Mah-Jongg tiles clicked, as did Tom Mix at the box office, along with Pearl White, Harold Lloyd, the Gishes. Then, just as actresses gained respectability(the screen put distance between the flesh and the road), the first Miss America graced Atlantic City's boardwalk to the tune of "Ma, He's Makin' Eyes at Me." Winners too were chocolate-coated Eskimo Pies, Flaherty's landmark documentary *Nannook of the North.* Playwright Eugene O'Neill, single-handedly, changed the direction of American theater—inward—with painful psychological dramas. Seeds sown years earlier by Carver and Burbank blossomed in print—*Better Homes and Gardens.* Radicals hung on every word in Menchen and Nathan's *American Mercury.* Humor, filtered through John Held, Jr., took a brassier turn in an age of jazz babies, college humorists, and flappers.

Flaming youth created a whole new image from head to toe. Females: bobbed hair, bobby pins, headache bands, cloches, bound bosoms, step-ins, chemises, costume jewelry, flesh-colored hose, pointed strap sandals, spectator pumps, and the newest footwear, flapping galoshes, from whence came *flapper.* They kissed

naturalism goodbye with lipstick, rouge, powder, nail polish, and permanent (waved by Frankenstein machine); at mushrooming salons, gyms, beauty parlors, and success schools, they willingly molded themselves into "It" girls. Sporty sidekicks slicked down hair, wore Harold Teen hats, racoon coats, bell bottoms (complete with hip flask), argyle socks, and saddle shoes. Together they sang "Who Cares?" to the strum of a uke and Charlestoned till dawn. They were the "cat's meow" with "lots of get up and go"—just two of the smart, slangy expressions dropped over dial phones. The country, sobered momentarily by Harding's

death, was shortly to reel with Teapot Dome. Tin Pan Alley's favorite was "Tea for Two." Voters of Wyoming and Texas elected Nellie Ross and Ma Ferguson the first women governors the year (1924) Americans chose between "Coolidge or chaos." J. Edgar Hoover was promoted to FBI chief; Clarence Darrow, the loser to William Jennings Bryan in Scopes's "monkey trial," won life for Leopold and Loeb, on trial for the murder of Bobby Franks.

The "new morality" spawned lurid motion pictures (De Mille's *Ten Commandments* an exception), sex magazines, *True Story, True Confessions,* whose publishers skillfully aroused the reader, not the censor. Caviar sophisticates ate up Harold Ross's *New Yorker;* the real-estate hungry, Florida land. Pet lovers preferred the police dog (glamorized by Rin Tin Tin); theatergoers, the perennial *Abie's Irish Rose;* bigtimers, Mae West, Ed Wynn, Sophie Tucker, the chorus lines of Earl Carroll. Spectator sportsmen cheered Knute Rockne's Four Horsemen and Channel swimmer Gertrude Ederle. Aimee Semple McPherson, mixing sex, sawdust, and soul, created the International Church of the Foursquare Gospel; contract overtook auction bridge; the black bottom vied with the Charleston; "Bye Bye Blackbird," with "Someone to Watch Over Me." Playwright Maxwell Anderson's *What Price Glory* and poet e.e. cummings's *Enormous Room,* two distillations of World War I, devastated many. Poetry lovers read Frost, Masters, and Robinson; Millay, Lowell, and Stein; Lindsay and Sandburg, whose *Abraham Lincoln: The Prairie Years* was published in '26. Willa Cather returned to the prairie, Edith Wharton and Ellen Glasgow to vanishing aristocracies (North and South). If Fitzgerald and Hemingway spoke for the "lost generation," Ferber and Hurst spoke to popular taste. Kids read *The Bobsey Twins* and *The Hardy Boys*; critical adults, the agonizing *American Tragedy* of Dreiser and the social dissections of Lewis, his fictitious *Arrowsmith* matched in excitement by de Kruiff's nonfiction *Microbe Hunters*.

By the twenties, modern medicine was in full swing. Disease was attacked by bacteriologists, chemists, doctors, and medical scholars; country doctors left behind by city specialists and clinics. Fading fast were unlimited house calls, home care for the seriously ill, childbirth outside hospitals. Spearheading the new medicine, a dramatic proliferation of research projects, laboratories, medical schools, and hospital facilities. Flourishing too, though fairly new on the scene, were growing numbers of chiropractors, osteopaths, and geneticists. Life spans lengthened and death rates dropped—yellow fever, smallpox, diphtheria, typhus conquered; pellagra, hookworm, malaria, treatable. Vitamin E was isolated, the iron lung invented, neurological surgery improved, pediatrics established. Infant mortality declined along with breast-feeding on demand and Victorian upbringing—much love and no nonsense. The flapper's baby, born with anesthetic, was bottle-fed on schedule à la behaviorist Watson—crying was in; cuddling out. Testers invaded schools, in quest of IQ's, and industry, in quest of data to hire and fire. The tantalizing art of psychiatry was to lure the rich or highly vulnerable to the psychoanalyst's couch, the new panacea. More common were asylums, dark places prevalent until the Menningers of Kansas shed new light.

In New Mexico, Robert Goddard got rocketry off the ground, where it stayed until the guiding direction of Sperry's gyroscope came some years later. *Seventh Heaven* gave Janet Gaynor the first Oscar (1927) as radio assumed the role of communicator, channeling help to seven hundred thousand flood sufferers. In the same year, sports fans watched Dempsey downed by Tunney, Ty Cobb eclipsed by Babe Ruth, swatting sixty homers. Lucky Lindy flew the *Spirit of St. Louis* nonstop New York to Paris, given there a hero's welcome and here a ticker tape parade, a key to the city, by New York's dandy little mayor Jimmy Walker.

At the Algonquin's Round Table rapier wits parried: Dorothy Parker, Robert Benchley, and Robert Sherwood, later joined by Margaret Case Harriman, Charles MacArthur, Ben Hecht, Franklin P. Adams. Many intellectuals and artists, having fought valiantly, laid reputations on the line for Sacco and Vanzetti but sadly saw them electrocuted (their guilt

very much in doubt). Isadora Duncan, interpretative dancer with innovative life-style, was strangled grotesquely by her own scarf while motoring. News zipped around the Times tower, *The Front Page* and *Good News* opened on Broadway, Mickey Mouse scampered across the screen, Al Jolson made history in *The Jazz Singer*. George Bellows, Edward Hopper, and Walt Kuhn painted realistically; Peter Blume, surrealistically; Georgia O'Keeffe, abstractly; while Gutsom Borglum supersculpted Mount Rushmore. Brick and glass faced the architecture of cities; stucco, the suburban bungalow; historic stone, the Mediterranean extravaganzas of Hearsts and Posts.

In an epoch of bad manners, Emily Post frowned on those "Makin' Whoopee," the "Let's Do It" crowd: flagpole sitters, Brooklyn Bridge jumpers, six-day bikers. The crossword-puzzle craze primed dictionary sales; bestsellers before the Great Crash; Thorne Smith's *Topper*, Marquis's *archy and mehitabel*, the first Ellery Queen, the latest Hemingway, Faulkner, and Thomas Wolfe. Hoover rode into office with "A chicken in every pot, a car in every garage." As people sang "Great Day," a Miami housewife gave birth on a plane; the Museum of Modern Art opened to the public; Elmer Rice's *Street Scene*, to critical acclaim. The scene on Wall Street closed with a resounding crash—some brokers drowning in ticker tape, others jumping out windows.

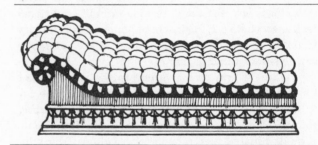

The wonder children of the twenties, the radio and the car, broke down old patterns into new life-styles —the "tin lizzie" transforming a horse-and-buggy land into a modern mobile nation. Ideas, like the car, now mass-produced through the media (radio, magazines, syndicated news services) homogenized life-styles from coast to coast. The development, slow and uneven, was faster in cities than on farms; in the city, few sewers; in the country, a privy in the back, water from a well; and in both, carpets cleaned by vacuum, Model T's (bought on installment) at the door. The yard shrank, through the lawn a path cut to the garage, the porch used less for work than courting in the swing. Exteriors of houses went from ornate to plain; interiors, from spacious to compact, closets becoming bathrooms. Diminished space—spare bedrooms and parlors, casualties—was to end the extended family, beginning the nuclear family—old folks eventually excluded. The keynote of homes was livableness; for those able to afford them, electric appliances, telephones, central heating were musts.

Women's time in the kitchen was diminished by more food stores, delicatessens, fresh fruits and vegetables year round, varieties of precooked foods, Birdseye's frozen ones, more and more packaged staples. The cracker barrel disappeared and with it the philosophy.

With the car, country restaurants sprang up along roads, farm wives catered to "joy-riders," traditional mealtimes changed. High-school lunchrooms, factory cafeterias, men's clubs caused vacant places at table; even leisurely Sunday dinners were going. A typical evening might find mother glued to the radio, father at a lodge meeting, daughter and boyfriend in the car on their way to the movies (the new courting grounds), and son off to basketball practice. Team sports dominated high schools; curriculums from kindergarten up had more frills, less authoritarianism. Solo and group singing assumed new importance in high schools as well as in adult groups—civic, business, or labor. Parlor singing and serenading, drowned out by phonograph and radio, now belonged to the past.

For many, the musical and social blast of the year was the chatauqua tent show, an American institution serving up culture, education, and fun: brass bands, opera divas, orchestras, yodelers, magicians, even lecturers extolling the glories of personal success. The era of the tent held up as long as the economy, collapsing along with everything else.

Investments made by the previous century's musical missionaries matured when public-school music programs led to greater demands for training at higher levels. State universities created music departments; Eastman, Curtis, and Juilliard endowed. Until World War I, an American musical life rooted in colonial singing schools grew in cities with settlement music classes—music viewed as social advancement among immigrant poor. Workingmen learned to read notes, joining choruses in communal or professional settings; the emphasis on native song. Musical groups outgrew school and neighborhood to become semiprofessional choruses and municipal concert societies; outdoor festivals brought music to the masses (Hollywood Bowl in California, Lewisohn Stadium in New York), discarding the hurly-burly carnival atmosphere of the tent show.

During the war, Tin Pan Alley patriotism, not folk music, was the dominant voice: "Over There," "I'm a Yankee Doodle Dandy," "I Didn't Raise My Boy to Be a Soldier." Enormously popular too were parodies of hit songs; one of the funniest, "K.P. Kitchen Police" ("K-K-K-Katy, Beautiful Katy"), the work of spirited doughboys with a never-ending string of "Hinky-Dinky" verses.

Postwar conductors dished up potpourri programs with a sprinkling of American composers: Hill, Mason, Griffith, and Carpenter (very Anglo-European), experimental Cowell, folkloristic Copland, jazzy Gershwin. An American musical idiom was clearly emerging; its strongest base—jazz.

Inside barrelhouses, pianos ragged the blues; outside, bands jazzed up spirituals or marches for parades and funerals. Early in the century, a handful of phonograph records introduced Dixieland to the nation; with the war, black soldiers and jazz performers took it to Europe. In the twenties,  radio picked it up and rode the black population shift north, from country to city; the audible impact of jazz marked by the pseudo-jazz of Paul Whiteman and the world premiere of Gershwin's *Rhapsody in Blue* (1924). White musicians, trying to satisfy the Roaring Twenties' passion for dancing, literally took over the air waves: Vincent Lopez, Ted Weems, Ted Lewis, Rudy Vallee. Tin Pan Alley blew up a storm, piping free entertainment into the parlor. As radio zoomed, record sales dipped, to be boosted back up by the dance-music craze, plus mounting demand for pure black music—mainly blues not heard on radio. In demand were city blues waxed by Mamie Smith, Ma Rainey,

Ida Cox, and Bessie Smith, so popular her disks sold out the moment they hit the Chicago ghetto or Harlem.

Small combos of southern musicians found a ready market for music they'd left behind: Jelly Roll Morton's Hot Peppers' "Black Bottom Stomp" and "Jelly Roll Blues"; King Oliver's Creole Jazz Band's "Snake Rag"; Satchmo Armstrong's Hot Five's "Gut Bucket Blues" and "Muskrat Ramble." Father of them all was W.C. Handy, with "Memphis" and "St. Louis Blues." But the free improvisations of the combo were to force a new development; arranged jazz for the big band, pioneered by Fletcher Henderson. With Duke Ellington came orchestral refinement, lushness of style—"The Mooche" and "Black and Tan Fantasy." So appealing, so popular was the sound that by mid-decade the period was being called the Jazz Age. Record companies, recognizing a rough diamond, lost no time dragging newly portable equipment (as did their serious counterparts, the folk song collectors) through southern barrelhouse, prison cell, and riverside shanty for nuggets of pure folk blues. Up north, Tin Pan Alley's arrangers polished them into slick commercial products, elegant and expensive as the people who danced to them in ballrooms and on rooftops of ritzy hotels.

Although lumped under one label, the primitive originals and the sophisticated copies were two very different types of music. Early jazz, a synthesis of the march dance beat overlaid with the syncopation of rags and the free-form expression of various black song styles—the repetitive chantlike work song, the solitary field holler, the religious spiritual, the secular blues—saw the innovative transfer from voice to instrument and instrument to instrument; the trumpet replacing the mellower cornet; the guitar, the banjo; the string bass, the tuba of the brass band.

The two most fertile elements to capture the tremors of the time, with all its wild contradictions, were the blues and the protest song, straight from the people closest to the ground shift—black and white field and factory hands. Out of the cotton field came "Pick a Bale of Cotton" and the humorous "Boll Weevil." Sharecroppers and tenant farmers complained "Down on Penny's Farm" about "11-cent Cotton, 40-cent Meat." Rural blues ached with the fears and fantasies of "Joe Turner," "The St. James Infirmary," and "Midnight Special"; city blues, the violence of "Frankie and Johnny." If there were "Hard Times in the Mill" down south, "The Poor Working Girl" had hers up north, where picket lines produced protest songs both lyrical and militant: "On the Line," "Bread and Roses," "Pie in the Sky." Making less of a noise at the time, their music's virile strain was destined to outlive Tin Pan Alley's manufactured species.

Boll Weevil

Traditional

Wisely

A   **Ama7**   **F#m**   **A**   **Dma7**

mf
1. The boll wee-vil is a lit-tle black bug, Came from Mex-i-co, they
2. The first time I seen a boll wee-vil He's a-sit-tin' on the

A   **F7**   **A**   **Bm/A**

say,
square;   All the way to Tex-as Just a-
Next time I seen the wee-vil He had

Amaj7   **D**   **A**   **Am6**   **E7**

look-in' for a place to stay. Just a-look-in' for a home,
all his fam-'ly there. Just a-look-in' for a home,

p lightly

A

Just a-look-in' for a home,   *f* Just a-look-in' for a
Just a-look-in' for a home,   Just a-look-in' for a

home,   Just a-look-in' for a home. _____
home,   Just a-look-in' for a home. _____

3. The farmer said to the weevil,
 "What makes your head so red?"
 The boll weevil said to the farmer,
 "It's a wonder I ain't dead.
  Just a-lookin' for a home. . . ."

4. The farmer took the weevil
 And shoved him in hot sand;
 The weevil said to the farmer,
 "I'll stand it like a man.
  It'll be my home. . . ."

5. The farmer took the weevil
 And set him on the ice;
 The boll weevil said to the farmer,
 "This is cool and mighty nice.
  It'll be my home. . . ."

6. The farmer took the weevil
 And fed him on Paris Green;
 The weevil said to the farmer,
 "That's the best I've ever seen.
  It'll be my home. . . ."

7. The boll weevil said to the farmer,
 "You'd better leave me alone;
 I et up all your cotton
 And now I'll eat your corn.
  I'll have a home. . . ."

8. The farmer said to the merchant,
 "We're in an awful fix;
 The boll weevil et all the cotton up
 And lef' us only sticks.
  We got no home. . . ."

9. The merchant got half the cotton,
 The weevil got the rest;
 Didn't leave the farmer's wife
 But one old calico dress.
  And it's full of holes. . . .

10. And if anybody should ax you
 Who was it writ this song,
 It was the farmer man,
 With all but his ov'ralls gone,
  Just a-lookin' for a home. . . .

Midnight Special

Traditional

3. Yonder comes my sweet Roberta. Ask me how do I know.
   That's the color of her apron and the dress she wo';
   Her unbrella's on her shoulder; got a paper in her hand.
   She goes right up to the captain, says, "Turn me loose, my man." [*Refrain*]

4. I'm a-goin' away and leave you; and the time ain't long.
   The captain's gonna call me, and I'll be goin' home.
   I'll be done with all my grievin', weepin', whoopin', and cryin';
   I'll be done with my worryin', 'bout my great, long time. [*Refrain*]

No More Cane on This Brazos

Traditional

3. Oughta come on the river in Nineteen Four. Oh—
   You could find a dead man on every turn row. Oh—

4. Oughta come on the river in Nineteen Ten. Oh—
   They was drivin' the women just like the men. Oh—

5. Oh, wake up, dead man, help me drive my row. Oh—
   Now, wake up, dead man, help me drive my row. Oh—

6. You wake up, lifer, and hold up your head. Oh—
   You may get pardon or you may drop dead. Oh—

7. Go down, Old Hannah, don't you rise today. Oh—
   If you rise this morning, bring that Judgment Day. Oh—

Hard Times in the Mill

Vigorously

Traditional

3. Ev'ry mornin' at six o'clock,
Two cold biscuits, hard as a rock. [*Refrain*]

4. Ev'ry mornin' at half-past nine,
The boss is cussin' and the spinners cryin'. [*Refrain*]

5. They docked me a nickel; they docked me a dime;
They sent me to the office to get my time. [*Refrain*]

6. Cotton-mill boys don't make enough
To buy tobacco or a pinch of snuff. [*Refrain*]

7. Ev'ry night when I get home,
A piece of cornbread and an old hambone. [*Refrain*]

8. Ain't it enough to break your heart,
Workin' ev'ry night till it's plumb dark? [*Refrain*]

Pie in the Sky

Words by *Joe Hill*
Music: Traditional

glo - ri - ous land in the sky; Work and play, live on
(work and play)

hay, You'll eat pie in the sky when you die."
(live on hay)

3. Holy Rollers and Jumpers come out.
   How they holler and jump and do shout:
   "Give your money to Jesus," they say,
   "He'll cure all the illness today." [*Chorus*]

4. Well sir, I for one want my pie now.
   How dare some preacherman raise a row?
   It ain't my soul that craves food this day,
   But my sick stomach growling away. [*Chorus*]

5. If you fight hard for children and wife,
   Try to get something good in this life.
   You're a sinner and bad man, they tell,
   When you die, you will sure go to hell. [*Chorus*]

6. Working men of all countries, unite!
   Side by side, we for freedom will fight.
   When the world and its wealth we have gained,
   To the grafters we'll sing this refrain: [*Chorus*]

Alternate
Chorus: You will eat (you will eat) by and by (by and by)
        When you've learned how to cook and to fry (way up high).
        Chop some wood (chop some wood), do you good (do you good),
        And you'll eat in the sweet by and by. (That's no lie.)

Frankie and Johnny

Traditional

[148]

3. Frankie went down to the barroom
   Just to buy a bucket of beer.
   She said to the big bartender,
   "Has my lovin' man been here?
       He is my man; he wouldn't do me wrong."

4. "Ain't gonna tell you no story.
   Ain't gonna tell you no lie.
   Your Johnny left here an hour ago
   With a gal called Allie Fly.
       He is your man, but he's doin' you wrong."

5. Frankie went back to the hotel.
   She didn't go there for no fun,
   For under her red kimono
   Was a forty-four caliber gun.
       Johnny was her man, and he was doin' her wrong.

6. Frankie looked over the transom.
   What she saw was no surprise.
   There on a couch was her Johnny
   Makin' love to that Allie Fly.
       He was her man, and he was doin' her wrong.

7. First time she shot him, he staggered.
   Next time she shot him, he fell.
   Third time she shot him—Lord Jesus!—
   There was a new man's face in hell.
       She shot her man, 'cause he was doin' her wrong.

8. The sheriff came round in the mornin',
   Said, "It was all for the best.
   That no-good, two-faced Johnny
   Was a nuisance and a pest.
       He was your man, and he done you wrong."

9. Bring on your two-wheel barouches;
   Bring on your rubber-tired hack.
   Seven goin' down to the graveyard;
   Only six are comin' back.
       He was her man, but he done her wrong.

10. This story, it has no moral,
    Just as it has no end.
    It only goes to show you
    That there ain't no good in men.
        He was her man, but he done her wrong.

Around Her Neck She Wore a Yellow Ribbon

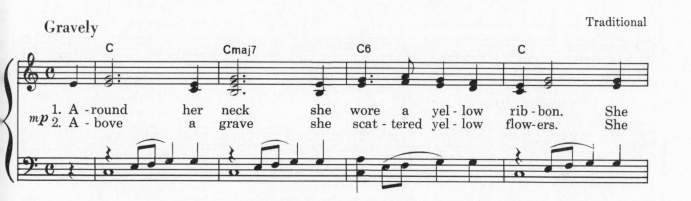

Gravely

Traditional

C   Cmaj7   C6   C

mp

1. A - round   her neck   she wore   a yel - low   rib - bon.   She
2. A - bove   a grave   she scat - tered yel - low   flow - ers.   She

The Poor Working Girl

Traditional

Sadly

mp

1. The poor work-ing girl, may hea-ven pro-tect her, She has such an aw-f'ly hard time. ____ The rich man's daugh-ter goes haugh-ti-ly by. My God, do you won-der at crime? ____

2. The poor work-ing girl, the sweat-shop's hand-maid-en, Could do with some real peace of mind; ____ Too bad, her man drives his new mo-del T And drinks rot-ten hootch till he's blind. ____

Hinky Dinky Parlay-Voo!

Traditional

Joyously

1. Mad' - moi - selle from Ar - men - tières; par - lay-
M. P.'s say they won the war; par - lay-
med - ics, they can hold the line; par - lay-

voo? Mad' - moi - selle from Ar - men - tières;
voo? The M. P.'s say they won the war;
voo? The med - ics, they can hold the line;

par - lay - voo? Mad' - moi - selle from
par - lay - voo? The M. P.'s say they
par - lay - voo? The med - ics, they can

Ar - men - tières Nev - er heard of un - der - wear.
won the war Stand - ing guard at the Ca - fé d'Or.
hold the line With C. C. pills and i - o - dine.

non legato, like a tuba

cresc.

Hink - y dink - y par - lay - voo!

ff

F   D7   G7   C7(♭9)   1. 2.   F

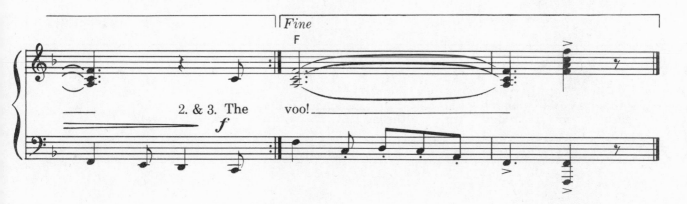

Fine

F

2. & 3. The   voo!

f

4. The tank boys claim they fought *très bon*; parlay-voo?
   The tank boys claim they fought *très bon*; parlay-voo?
   The tank boys claim they fought *très bon*
   Against the M.P.'s at Dijon.
      Hinky dinky parlay-voo!

5. The Horse Marines will do it all; parlay-voo?
   The Horse Marines will do it all; parlay-voo?
   The Horse Marines will do it all,
   Shooting crap in an empty stall.
      Hinky dinky parlay-voo!

6. And the story in the Signal Corps; parlay-voo?
   And the story in the Signal Corps; parlay-voo?
   And the story in the Signal Corps
   Is blackjack on the office floor.
      Hinky dinky parlay-voo!

7. The officers get all the steak; parlay-voo?
   The officers get all the steak; parlay-voo?
   The officers get all the steak;
   All we get is a belly ache.
      Hinky dinky parlay-voo!

8. The general got a Croix de Guerre; parlay-voo?
   The general got a Croix de Guerre; parlay-voo?
   The general got a Croix de Guerre;
   The son-of-a-bitch was never there!
      Hinky dinky parlay-voo!

9. The English call it a lovely war; parlay-voo?
   The English call it a lovely war; parlay-voo?
   The English call it a lovely war;
   Then what the hell are we fighting for?
      Hinky dinky parlay-voo!

When the Saints Go Marching In

Traditional

3. And when they crown Him King of Kings. . . .

4. And on that Hallelujah Day. . . .

5. And when the saints go marching in. . . .

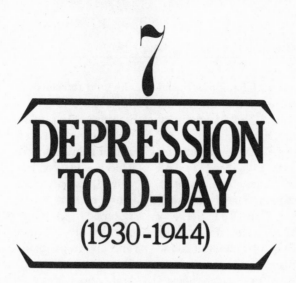

7
DEPRESSION TO D-DAY
(1930-1944)

The remarkable journey of the United States from bankruptcy to prosperity, isolationism to world leadership, from the depth of depression to the pinnacle of power—in fifteen short years—is an American success story par excellence. It began with banks, schools, and factories closed; unemployment high; many homeless, roaming the country in search of nonexistent work, living on charity and handouts. Roosevelt and the New Deal started the nation on the road to recovery, but the journey was hard, made harder still by Dust Bowl and bitter labor struggles. Out of the agony came social and economic reforms—with them, new hope. No sooner had the country got going when World War II forced it out of isolation. Tooled up in record time for all-out war, expanding goods and services beyond belief, the United States was on its way to all-out victory. Small wonder so many songs from those stormy days express the despair and confusion, hopes and struggles of so many: The Depression had them "Wandering," eating "Beans, Bacon, and Gravy"; "Chilly Winds" blew them from the Dust Bowl; but "A New Wind A-Blowin'" renewed hope; on the picket line miners' women declared "I Am a Union Maid," on the battle line was a "Star Spangled Banner Waving Somewhere," and through all, an abiding faith in America's "Pastures of Plenty."

The rippling aftershock of the Crash slammed the doors of over thirteen thousand banks. In 1930, the year Luce founded *Fortune*, one bank alone lost four hundred thousand depositors. On the rise were the game Monopoly, the sport skiing (the first snow train packed to New Engalnd), miniature golf (whole families playing at being Bobby Jones), the play *Green Pastures*, a heavenly new hit as marriages not made in heaven could get counseling and look on "The Sunny Side of the Street." Sudddenly nurses' futures turned bright as Harlow's hair with airlines taking them on as stewardesses to fly "Beyond the Blue Horizon." Wiley Post and Jimmy Doolittle set new records in aviation; Sinclair Lewis in literature, the first American to win a Nobel. A genius think-tank (The Institute for Advanced Study) opened in Princeton, the Veterans Administration its doors. From Havana came the roll of the rhumba, in time sharing the dance floor with the conga kick, their Latin beats bouncing over airwaves as radio beamed over oceans, continents, and hemispheres and the public eavesdropped on Admiral Byrd in New Zealand talking to *Times* publisher Ochs in New York. Culbertson loomed over the bridge table; the George Washington Bridge, over the Hudson; the Empire State Building, over 34th Street, on the old site of the Waldorf, moved to Park Avenue, the new home of transients and residents, famous and infamous—Lucky Luciano among them, key figure with Anastasia and Genovese in the underworld hierarchy (later the Mafia). At ground level, city gangs like the Dead End Kids spread terror; crisscrossing the country, Dillinger, Pretty Boy Floyd, Bonnie and Clyde. The Scottsboro Boys were framed, lynchings inflamed, Faulkner's *Sanctuary* brought fame. The "Star Spangled Banner" became the national anthem; radio astronomy, a new science, as astronomers squinted at Pluto and kids the flights of Flash Gordon. On *The Good Earth* writer Pearl Buck picked up a Pulitzer; shopping women, Bisquick off the shelves. Churches had penny suppers and White Castles nickel hamburgers. Tin Pan Alley sold "Life Is Just a Bowl of Cherries"; people sold apples on corners or lined up for bread and soup. Urey's "heavy water" was concocted in the real lab, *Frankenstein* and *Dracula* in the movie lab.

The Lindbergh case filled front pages in 1932, forcing the adoption of the death penalty for kidnapping. The death of vaudeville saw the Palace close, Winchell's microphone open, along with Radio City.

Movie theaters enticed customers with bank nights and double bills—*Scarface* with *Dr. Jekyll and Mr. Hyde.* Out of a test tube came Vitamin C, out of obscurity Babe Didrikson, breaking four Olympic records for women. Desperate couples entered dance marathons, dance halls offered "Ten Cents a Dance," pinball machines gobbled coins, Chicago racketeers emptied pockets to the tune of $145 million. The theme song of the Bonus Army, "Brother, Can You Spare a Dime?," brought veterans to Washington. Joining the folks on *Tobacco Road*, an army of homeless found shelter in Hoovervilles (clusters of tar-papered shacks), midnight missions, flophouses, stationhouses, parks. Men, women, and children rode the rods— railroads adding boxcars for nonpaying passengers, air conditioning for paying ones. Things moved up: metal escalators, tractors on pneumatic tires, first-class mail—two to three cents. Hope resurfaced with the New Deal; Roosevelt was in by a landslide, the ring of his voice radiating confidence, a captivating cockiness right down to the jaunty angle of his cigarette holder. Cigarette ads invited women to smoke, new Bennington College intrigued them to learn. Great Books programs grabbed intellectuals, as did FDR, for his Brain Trust. Congress moved up future inaugurations from March to January and repealed Prohibition as the new president reassured the nation there was "nothing to fear but fear itself." Tinkering with society, not machines, was his talent, bombarding Congress in the first hundred days with bills that irreversibly altered American life. First off he declared a "bank holiday," then flooded Capitol Hill with an alphabet of legislation: CCC, AAA, TVA, NRA, PWA, NERA, NLRB. And he floored many by appointing Frances Perkins Secretary of Labor—the first woman to hold a cabinet post.

Nationwide birth and death statistics first appeared; Death Valley made a national park in '33. The Lone Ranger rode on the air, Roosevelt's "fireside chat" became a fixture—"My Friends" giving hope to millions. In the East the black community flocked to Father Divine's "heavens" for religion and the staff of life. Theologian Niebuhr called for a return to orthodoxy. Hemlines dropped to mid-calf, waistlines went in, Ruth Owen went to Norway, the first female ambassador. While reporters Dorothy Thompson and Anne O'Hare McCormick wrote their way to fame with anti-Hitler, anti-Mussolini pieces, Sally Rand fanned her way to fame at the Chicago Fair—little girls soon bouncing balls to "Sally Rand lost her fan, give it back, you nasty man." School bells didn't ring for over two million children that year; working children earned a dollar a week at most. Off

the gold standard, the country welcomed Busby Berkeley's *Gold Diggers of 1933*; college kids swallowed goldfish. Despite fifty million toothbrushes sold, few Americans brushed their teeth. Perry Mason began making millions for Erle Stanley Gardner; Benton, Curry, and Wood began painting farmers.

Millions of farmers, plagued by drought and dust, were on the move. With eleven thousand counties doomed from Kansas to Texas, the federal government (through the AAA) ordered fields plowed under and livestock reduced. They told farmers what and how much to plant or breed, instituted crop rotation, soil conservation, subsidies, and ever-normal granaries in an effort to stabilize agriculture.

With one out of six Americans seeking help by 1934, the government (state and federal) was forced into another private sector—social work—implementing modest social-welfare programs administered, more often than not, by out-of-work teachers. Anthropologist Ruth Benedict's *Patterns of Culture* was amplified by life itself, economics frequently forcing the reversal of male-female social roles. Cole Porter wrote "Anything Goes"; if anything, the opposite was true, with the Hays Office giving most movies a hard time, Shirley Temple's excepted. A duck called Donald tickled many, so did *Famous Funnies*, the first comic book, delicious fun along with frozen custards. Kids spun around corners on orange-crate skooters; Wallace Carothers spun out polymer 66 (nylon); and the first disk jockey, records. The chain-letter craze radiated from Denver, *Porgy and Bess* lit up the mar-

quee, lynchings went down, demagogue Huey Long was killed in Baton Rouge. Humorist Will Rogers with aviator Wiley Post fatally crashed in Alaska as Pan Am's China Clipper winged across the Pacific. The upper class switched to planes from cars; for the business class the car was a habit, a pleasure; for the migrant, wheels to the future; for the working class, status—increasingly denied by work.

Lewis pulled out of Green's AFL craft union to form the industrial CIO. In 1935 Uncle Sam put millions of unskilled to work building parkways, public playgrounds, bathing facilities, golf courses, skating rinks (ice and roller), post offices. The WPA put artists to work painting murals; the FSA, photographers photographing "the forgotten man"; the Writers' Project, writers writing guide books, analyzing public problems. The Theater Project took theater to the people, community theater; the Music Project subsidized performers, composers, music education, lending libraries. Independently, yet collectively, each group brought social realism to its height—criticizing society, idealizing the common man—sometimes political, sometimes apolitical. Some called it proletarian art, others propaganda art.

"One Man's Family" captured listeners; Margaret Mead's *Sex and Temperament*, readers; Alcoholics Anonymous, problem drinkers—just about the time beer cans were invented. Adman Benton found out what the consumer wanted, Gallup did the polling, *Ballyhoo* magazine mocked it. Fewer clothes or no clothes showed up in nudist colonies, on beaches, in backyards. Suntans were in fashion; fake ones from corner drugstores, the influence of Hollywood, as the Westmores magnified the makeup market. Fred and Ginger were magnets at the box office; Ginger's slim lines a boost to the corset industry (a record sixty-seven million sales); the hydraulic lift to farmers; the first forecast center, to those in the hurricane belt. Both DAR and American Legion pressed nineteen state legislatures for loyalty oaths from teachers. Politically fervent youth joined the American Student Union; those seeking education and work, the NYA (National Youth Administration).

In 1935 Roosevelt signed the Social Security Act, the next year American gold was securely stored in Fort Knox. A healthier economy beefed up bank accounts, reflected in the building industry. $10,000 bought a lot of house—Tudor or Colonial. With increased leisure the yard got more use—sandbox, badminton, glider. With increased facilities more people enjoyed athletic programs, swimming pools, crafts, every kind of dancing. CCC instructors taught thirty-five thousand illiterates to read and write. Dale Carnegie explained *How to Win Friends and Influence People*, John Gunther went *Inside Europe*, Margaret Mitchell's *Gone with the Wind* took the country by storm. The management-labor storm shifted directions with the first sitdown strike, violence the result. Floods from rivers on the rampage found towns submerged, people perched on rooftops. Nevada was dry, the Colorado checked by Hoover Dam. Baseball had a hall of fame in Cooperstown when lights for the first night game went on; Bobby Riggs sprang over the net as clay-court tennis champ; black U.S. track star Jesse Owens won at the Olympics in Hitler's Germany. One hundred sixty thousand trailers crawled along roads; someone invented the parking meter; inventive Chaplin, *Modern Times. Automation* came into the language along with "knock knock" jokes. Roosevelt stayed on in the White House, but

King Edward left Buckingham Palace for "the woman I love"—both events flashed worldwide by AP wirephoto in 1936 and featured in *Life,* the new picture weekly.

Café society, the creation of press agents and gossip columnists, a Hollywood–Broadway–Park Avenue blend, starred Brenda Frazier in strapless gowns. The star in boxer trunks, Brown Bomber Joe Louis; in the funnies, Joe Palooka; at home plate, Joe DiMaggio; in the cockpit, Howard Hughes. Lost over the Pacific, aviatrix Amelia Earhart; in flames over Lakehurst, the Hindenburg. Congress defeated FDR's court-packing plan, the court ruled tapped conversations confidential. Neilsen ratings ruled the radio dial; sassy Charlie McCarthy lorded it over Edgar Bergen; Father Coughlin, opponents to his share-the-wealth plan with anti-Semitic overtones. The Good Neighbor Policy brought the Americas closer, the Neutrality Act fostered isolation.

By 1938 two out of three Americans were well fed, clothed, and sheltered. More people woke to alarm clocks than crowing roosters. Bathrooms, more compact, bright with colored tile, had legless tubs, stall showers, electric razors. Kitchens had less warmth,

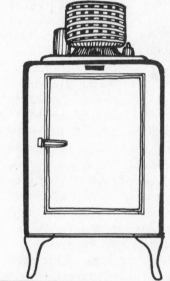

less clutter, more storage space, more efficiency: electrical appliances, easy-to-mop floors, asphalt tile. Available too were wall-to-wall carpeting, venetian blinds, tubular furniture, foam-rubber padding, mirrored walls, coffee tables, automatic record players. In the attached garage, a car with automatic transmission, without rumble seat or running board—the innovative station wagon running on high octane gas. Buses took kids to school, men to work, women shopping, the family to town. Main Streets were lined with chain stores, streamlined mom-and-pop shops, cafeterias, greasy spoons, corner bars, drugstores, and cigar stores; movie palaces, poolrooms, bowling alleys, a few supermarkets and discount houses. A nickel bought cupcakes, candy, coffee, a Coke, the paper, or a phone call. Permanents were 75¢; tuxes, rentable; corsages, badges for special occasions. Mothers and daughters bought tulle formals, juliet caps, berets, box coats, angora sweaters, swing skirts, dirndls, and petticoats; halters, shorts, slacks, culottes, playsuits, and sunglasses; maternity clothes, housecoats, anklets, spike heels, and saddle shoes. Men chose suits with wide lapels—seersucker in summer, pinstriped wool in winter—slacks, sports shirts, jackets belted in back, raincoats, snap-brimmed fedoras, earmuffs, and Windbreakers. Boys wore parkas, snowsuits, "whistle britches" (corduroy pants and knickers), polo shirts, G-man underwear, Mickey Mouse watches, and high tennis shoes.

After school, kids wolfed down Dagwood sandwiches, read comics, switched stations from hillbilly or soap opera to "Jack Armstrong, All-American Boy"—

little sisters elbow-deep in finger paint, brothers flying model planes or toying with premiums from cereal boxes. Somedays, they went to group music lessons (25¢ an hour), rehearsals, choir practice, or team practice. Evenings, Floyd Gibbons dramatized news, Kaltenborn analyzed news. Drama, comedy, variety, suspense, gossip, and music crowded the airwaves: Crosby, Cantor, Benny, Burns and Allen; Hedda, Louella, "Gangbusters" and "Information, Please." Weekends, opera, symphony, and barn dance were broadcast, and special reports, sportscasts—a thrilling moment when Budge won his fourth tennis crown. Downstairs were bridge, pinochle, and cigars; upstairs, pajama parties, pillow fights, metal curlers, and girltalk: boys were "smooth," girls "neat," everything "copacetic." Kids went steady or played the field in teen hangouts, bleachers (cheerleaders pom-poming them on), ice or roller rinks, necked in balconies (interrupted by intermissions for March of Dimes appeals). For youngsters the Saturday-afternoon movie was a ritual, for grown-ups bingo, for the whole family Sunday dinner out with music piped in.

Regular vacations became more of a reality when Congress put a ceiling over hours, a floor under wages, and limitations on child labor. Some people stayed home and fixed up the house, others visited relatives. Families piled into station wagons and headed for mountains or seashore. More kids went to camp, more parents took cruises and trips—the ultimate for many, riding the Superchief to Hollywood. There, a tour of the studios was a must; on the big stage at MGM, *The Wizard of Oz*; on the drawing board at Disney, *Fantasia*; *Snow White* already in theaters. Another must, a gawking ride past the homes of stars from Carole Lombard to Clark Gable, Norma Shearer to Spencer Tracy. In New York at *Our Town* and *Hellzapoppin'*, audiences beat their palms the night Orson Welles panicked millions at home with "The War of the Worlds" (a Martian-invasion hoax); listeners jittery from the real threat of war jammed switchboards and roads.

Factories were jammed with war orders. Prosperity seemed around the corner. War was unthinkable, not inevitable. Anti-German, anti-Italian feelings ran high; strict neutrality was a problem. The atom was split, Einstein urged Roosevelt to develop the bomb, DDT and nylons went on sale. In '39, both New York and San Francisco had fairs, projecting Americans into the future; their emphasis, technology (TV demonstrated). Both had aquacades; in the East, Eleanor Holm; in the West, Esther Williams. This was the year of the pocket book—the first, *Lost Horizons*; the price, 25¢. Sandburg's *Abraham Lincoln*: *The War Years* appeared as black contralto Anderson (barred from Constitution Hall) sang on the steps of the Lincoln Memorial. Archibald MacLeish appointed librarian of Congress, the first poet so honored. Sam Rayburn rose to Speaker of the House, the gavel his for decade upon decade.

In 1940 Congress passed the first peacetime draft—some two out of five draftees rejected quickly absorbed by war-swollen industries. The first Social Security checks went out, illiteracy down; down in the mines, thirteen thousand casualties. Steinbeck's *Grapes of Wrath* earned him a Pulitzer; black author Wright's *Native Son*, acclaim; FDR, the voters' acclaim for an unprecedented third term—the election returns heard in 30 million homes by most of America's 132 million. Isolationists said, "America First!"; refugees, "America, at last!" *The Great Dictator* made Hitler and Mussolini ridiculous; young musicians made music in Stokowski's new Youth Orchestra; the buzz overhead made by Sikorsky's new helicopter and planes making instrument landings. Technology took a giant step with the automatic sequence computer and electron microscope.

Penicillin and babies (the birth rate hitting a ten-year high) were mass-produced, as were radiant heating, aerosol sprays, plastics (replacing so many things). People went gin-rummy crazy, critics raved over

Welles's *Citizen Kane* and Agee's *Let Us Now Praise Famous Men.* Roosevelt and Churchill hammered out the Atlantic Charter restating the Four Freedoms. Lend-Lease flowed as controls were clamped on prices (OPA), production (WPB), information (OWI). The news of Pearl Harbor exploded like a bombshell all over America; the rallying cry, "Praise the Lord and Pass the Ammunition." From London, the voices of Shirer and Murrow, heard amidst whistling bombs and screaming sirens. Alerted Americans altered life-styles with air drills, plane spottings, blackouts, brown-outs, rationing, and doing without. Confined in camps were Italians, Germans, pacifists, and Japanese-Americans; nisei soldiers later distinguished themselves in the European theater of war, but the irony was lost on most Americans.

Doolittle raided Tokyo; the navy coined *radar*; the army, *snafu.* A network of Manhattan Project physicists set off the first nuclear chain reaction in Chicago, engineered the A-bomb at Oak Ridge that exploded in a mushroom cloud over Los Alamos. As astronomers catalogued five hundred million stars, *Stars on Ice* glistened in arenas and folks sang "White Christmas." Close to five hundred burned to death in Boston's Coconut Grove nightclub; baseball lost Lou Gehrig, "Pride of the Yankees." *Private Hargrove* left his heart at the stagedoor canteen and got "Dear John" letters by V-mail.

Americans landed in North Africa, took and held Guadalcanal, a Halsey victory in 1942. *So Proudly We Hail,* saluting American nurses, inspired many women to enlist in WACS, WAVES, WASPS (ferrying bombers), and SPARS. Merchant marines grabbed for "Mae Wests" as eight million tons of Allied shipping were sunk. War costs—$8 billion per month—were barely offset by withholding taxes and warbond sales, but Kate Smith singing "God Bless America" did help fill the treasury. Pinups and Petty girls were treasured by GI's, Kilroy was there, Wilkie wanted "One World," Roosevelt circled the globe for peace: Casablanca (not with Bogart and Bergman), Moscow, and Teheran. Requisitions routed through seventeen miles of Pentagon corridors ordered everything from crew cuts to ballpoint pens, C rations to sulfa drugs. Saddled with the heaviest packs in history (eighty-four pounds), soldiers slogged through Italian mud; up front brought to home front through the special reporting of Ernie Pyle, the cartooning of Bill Mauldin—sadsacks Willie and Joe with all-purpose helmets. People avidly followed the action in both theaters in papers, picture weeklies (photos and paintings), newsreels, radio—news every hour on the hour.

Something else new for radio was a series on race relations narrated by black actor Canada Lee; in the theater, Robeson's *Othello*; on film, Lena Horne in *Stormy Weather.* Race riots rocked Detroit, Mobile, Beaumont, and Harlem. Bobby-soxers rioted, ripped up the Paramount on Broadway when "The Voice," Frank Sinatra, crooned "A Lovely Way to Spend an Evening." *Forever Amber* topped the bestseller list; horseracing was out for the duration; Helen Wills out for good, and Alice Marble was seeded #1. As twelve women sat in Congress, GI benefits were voted in for eleven million in uniform. Streptomycin and synthetic quinine saved lives; USO shows, variety personified, with starlets and stars (Bob Hope, Martha Raye) boosted morale of soldiers overseas; "Since You Went Away," of stateside civilians. Proof positive of victory in the making, a fifth star added to the insignias of admirals King, Leahy, and Nimitz, generals Arnold, Eisenhower, MacArthur, and Marshall by D-Day.

At home, Americans tightened belts, wallets grew fatter, unemployment evaporated (small pockets remained in the South), farmers never had it so good. Relocation strained housing and service facilities, creating boom towns. Nightclubs, juke joints jumped; with alcohol siphoned into industry, beer became the national drink. Women took to the wraparound skirt, tailored suit (shoulders padded), sequined cocktail dress, "chubby" fox jacket; hoarded nylons, two-way stretches, briefs, suede pumps. Civilian men, carefully combed pompadours under porkpie hats, wore cuffless, single-breasted suits, tie clips, pointed shoes, a sharp contrast to crew-cut servicemen in khaki and navy. Exempt from WPB restrictions were infants' wear, bridal gowns, maternity clothes, religious vestments, burial gowns. Americans bought everything in sight: boogie to birdcall records, tickets and books galore; library circulation spurted 15 percent. Home sewing, home canning, victory gardens all revived with the flash of a *V*. Hard to get were vacations, cigarettes, fuel, tires, metal toys, soap, sugar, coffee, flour, butter, and margarine with color pack to yellow it. Hard to take were high prices and waiting lines, even for dentists and doctors; the house call gone forever.

At work, pampering was in. Background music, coffee breaks, bowling leagues, self-improvement courses, fringe benefits: more life insurance, hospitalization, bonuses. Rosie the Riveter and Swing-Shift Mazie, some five million strong (out of seventeen million working women) built bombers and fighters, taking on heavier, more dangerous work than ever in history, forcing historic breakthroughs in child and health care. In the case of equal pay for equal work, no breakthrough; men paid three times better. From daybreak to backache, many women in snoods went from overalls to shirtwaist dresses as they managed households too.

Full-time housewives stoically coped with shortages and the dual-parent role, saved for the future, stocked closets with Sterno cans and first-aid kits. Women gave each other home permanents, mastered tools, did repairs. Military wives swung with improvised lifestyles, cooking on hot plates, using makeshift refrigeration, making new friends, moving around, moving back home, sometimes with babies.

The new phenomenon was the eight-hour orphan or latch-key kid roaming streets, locked in cars outside war plants—the breeding ground of delinquency as the peer group replaced the family. The uniform for boys, the zoot suit; for girls, the juke jacket; for both, saddle shoes or loafers. With lack of parental care premature sexuality thrived; jitterbugging often end-

ing in slugging free-for-alls. The teenage subculture surfaced, creating a new consumer market with kids spending lots on movies, faddist junk, and records, records, records.

Ellington's record "It Don't Mean a Thing If It Ain't Got That Swing" gave the name to a jazz style developed by black bands in the late twenties, but not in the groove till mid-thirties. Americans wanted soothing sounds: Rudy Vallee, Bing Crosby, Guy

Lombardo, and Wayne King. The swinging manner of the new jazz started catching on with radio's "Let's Dance"—really catching on the night Benny Goodman played the Palomar Ballroom. It was love at first sound; the teen-age crush immediate with jitterbugging in the aisles: the big apple, the lindy, the shag, the Suzy-Q. Tin Pan Alley swung too, with a runaway hit, "Goody, Goody." If Benny was king, the Count and the Duke were powers behind the throne, giving the era depth and momentum. White band leaders with easy access to mass audiences made swing the rage: the Dorseys, Artie Shaw, Glen Miller, first; Harry James, Woody Herman, Spike Jones, all-girl bands, later. Sidemen in the tradition of improvised jazz flew high over the arranged riffs of everything from Bach to boogie: hornmen Armstrong, Eldridge, and Gillespie; slidemen Teagarden and Johnson; on sax, Hawkins, Young, and Parker; licorice stick, Buddy deFranco; guitar, Charlie Christian; on skins, Gene Krupa; bass, Jimmy Blanton; 88's, Teddy Wilson breaking the color barrier with the Benny band, singer Billie Holliday with Artie Shaw. By '38 people jumped to, jived to, drank to, listened to combos or big bands really swinging.

Via New Orleans, Chicago, and Kansas City jazz blew into New York, "Stompin' at the Savoy," bouncing at the Cotton Club, headlining at the Apollo and Carnegie Hall. Little clubs lining 52nd Street mixed old and new, vocal and instrumental: Buster Bailey, Eddie Condon, John Kirby, Pee Wee Russell, Art Tatum, and Fats Waller. From soloist to single: Mildred Bailey, Billie Holliday, Ella Fitzgerald, Anita O'Day. Scat singing, beeps, bleeps, and chirps, after-hours jams explored new soundscapes: Dizzy Gillespie, Charlie ("Bird") Parker, Kenny Clarke; blue notes, contrapuntal inventions from the throats and hands of Hazel Scott and Mary Lou Williams.

In the early forties music turned back to Dixieland and "South of the Border." Samba dancers dislocated backs bumping along with bubbling Carmen Miranda or Cugie's ruffled crew. Marimbas, maracas, motion unlimited. Changing tastes were only part of the story; more to the point, big bands declined when a strike cut off new recordings, costs cut off road trips and radio revived New Orleans, played old standards, played up crooners and the sentimental ballad. Females swooned over Frank Sinatra, Dick Haymes, Perry Como, Billy Eckstine; female singers in demand: Dinah Shore, Jo Stafford, Ginny Simms, Sarah Vaughan. Rich strings schmaltzed the classics; making schmaltzy classics: André Kostelanetz, Ferde Grofé, Morton Gould, David Rose, Leroy Anderson. Movie scores came from Alfred Newman, Victor

Young, Meredith Willson, Bernard Herrmann.

Serious American music carved out an audience of its own. Conductors programmed Barber, Harris, Piston, and Still. Opera theaters performed Blitzstein, Gruenberg, Menotti. More versatile were Copland, Thomson, and Bernstein working with peers in ballet, De Mille and Robbins; modern dance, Graham and Humphrey; film, Lorentz and Flaherty; on Broadway, at the Met, in the concert hall; creating music for fast growing rosters of American singers, dancers, and instrumentalists.

Another stream was to turn musical comedy into musical theater: *Oklahoma!*, *Kiss Me Kate*, *On the Town*. Tunesmithing throughout the whole period: Gershwin, Kern, Porter, and Rodgers. Still another development, the jazzed-up opera and operetta: *Carmen Jones* and *Hot Mikado*.

Nashville's Grand Old Opry, not opera at all but there all the time, gave hillbilly song, dance, and country instruments a new twang. Sponsored by midwestern radio stations (road shows on the side) hillbilly bounced over hill and dale in the thirties. Sears and Ward made a killing selling cheap disks by mail. Headliners Jimmie Rodgers, Bill Monroe, Roy Acuff, the Carters, Hank Williams, and Tex Ritter put bluegrass on the map; Gene Autry and Roy Rogers put "cow-billy" on film.

At the grass roots nurturing America's folk heritage was a handful of singer-collectors carefully tending the garden that was to flower in the fifties. Hovering over the blues were the towering figures of Leadbelly, Big Bill Broonzey, Josh White. Listening, learning, expressing life's trials, tribulations, humor, and heartache were wandering minstrels Guthrie, Houston, Ives, and Seeger; providing strong material for migrant and miner were Sis Cunningham, Aunt Molly Jackson, and Florence Reece; for picket line, Garland and Glazer. Preserving material for posterity, Ben Botkin and the Lomaxes for the Library of Congress: for the public, Folkways Records; both netting now treasured songs before lost, transmuted, or corrupted.

Blues were sad, angry, humorous: "No Dough Blues," "Git Back Blues," "No Depression in Heaven." Struggles, hard, were they with beast ("Whoo, Back, Buck!"), boss ("I Don't Want Your Millions, Mister"), or nature ("Chilly Winds"). Folks sang "So Long, It's Been Good to Know Yuh" with wry resignation, "The TVA" with optimism, "Beans, Bacon, and Gravy" with carefree humor, "Cripple Creek" with rustic humor, and "Gathering Flowers for the Master's Bouquet" with perennial faith. Whatever the mood—mishap, misgiving, misery, or mirth—pride in America soared with "This Land Is Your Land."

So Long, It's Been Good to Know Yuh

Woody Guthrie

know yuh, So long, it's been good to know yuh;

So long, it's been good to know yuh. This dust-y old dust is a-

get-tin' my home, And I've got to be drift-in' a-long. _____

3. We talked on the end of the world, and then,
We'd sing a song, and then sing it again;
We'd sit for an hour and not say a word,
And then these words would be heard: [*Chorus*]

4. The sweethearts sat in the dark and they sparked.
They hugged and kissed in that dusty old dark.
They sighed and cried, hugged and kissed,
Instead of marriage they talked like this: Honey, [*Chorus*]

5. Now, the telephone rang and it jumped off the wall;
That was the preacher a-makin' his call.
He said, "Kind friend, this may be the end;
You've got your last chance of salvation of sin." [*Chorus*]

6. The churches was jammed, and the churches was packed,
And that dusty old dust storm blowed so black;
The preacher could not read a word of his text,
And he folded his specs and he took up collection, said: [*Chorus*]

Roll On, Columbia

Words by *Woody Guthrie*
Music based on "Goodnight Irene"
by *Huddie Ledbetter* ("*Leadbelly*")
and *John A. Lomax*

CHORUS

f Roll on, Co - lum - bia, roll on;
Roll on, Co - lum - bia, roll on. Your
pow - er is turn - ing our dark - ness to dawn, So
roll on, Co - lum - bia, roll on.

4. And on up the river is Grand Coulee Dam,
The mightiest thing ever built by a man;
To run the great factories and water the land,
It's roll on, Columbia, roll on! [*Chorus*]

5. These mighty men labored by day and by night,
Matching their strength 'gainst the river's wild flight;
Through rapids and falls they won the hard fight,
Roll on, Columbia, roll on. [*Chorus*]

Whoa, Back, Buck!

Huddie Ledbetter ("Leadbelly")
Edited with new material
by *John A.* and *Alan Lomax*

CHORUS 2

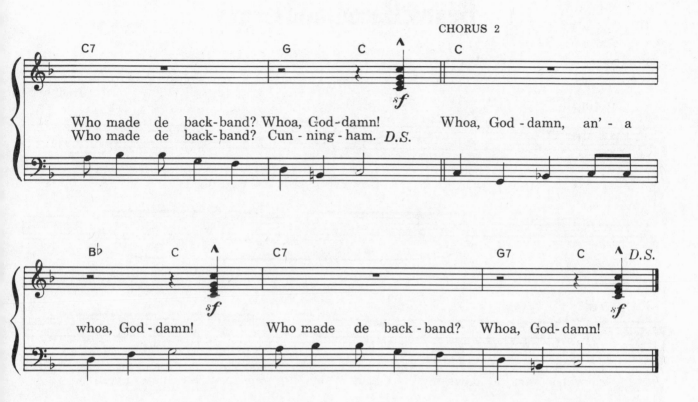

3. I taken Sal to de party-o,
   Eighteen, nineteen, twenty years ago,
   All dressed up in her calico;
   Wouldn't let her dance but a set or so. [Choruses 1 & 2]

4. Me an' my gal come a-walkin' down de road,
   Wind f'om her feet knockin' "Sugar in de Gou'd,"
   Sugar in de gou'd an' de gou'd on de groun',
   Want to get de sugar got to roll de gou'd aroun'. [Chorus 1]

5. Chicken in de bread-pan, mighty good stuff,
   Mamma cook him chicken an' he never get enough;
   Jawbone walk an'-a jawbone talk,
   Jawbone eat it wid a knife an' fork. [Choruses 1 & 2]

Beans, Bacon, and Gravy

Traditional

Brightly

1. I was born long a - go, in
2. We con - gre - gate each morn - ing At the

Eigh-teen Nine - ty - four, And I've seen man - y a pan - ic, I will
coun-try barn at dawn-ing And ev - 'ry - one is hap - py, so it

own. I've been hun - gry, I've been cold, And
seems. But when our work is done, We

now I'm grow-ing old But the worst I've seen is Nine-teen Thir - ty - nine.
file in one by one, And thank the Lord for one more mess of beans.

CHORUS

Oh, those beans, ba-con, and grav-y, They al-most drive me cra-zy. I eat them till I see them in my dreams, in my dreams. When I wake up in the morn-ing And an - oth - er day is dawn-ing, I know I'll have an - oth - er mess of beans.

We have Hooverized on butter,
For milk we've only water,
And I haven't seen a steak in many a day.
As for pies 'n cakes 'n jellies,
We substitute sowbellies,
For which we work the country road each day. [*Chorus*]

4. If there ever comes a time
When I have more than a dime,
They will have to put me under lock and key,
For I've been broke so long
I can only sing this song
Of the workers and their misery. [*Chorus*]

[171]

The TVA

Traditional

Cheerfully

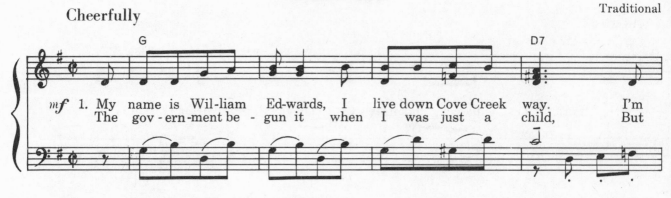

mf 1. My name is Wil-liam Ed-wards, I live down Cove Creek way. I'm
The gov-ern-ment be-gun it when I was just a child, But

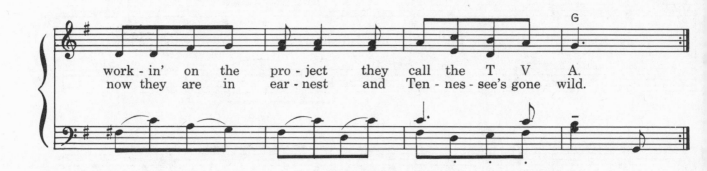

work-in' on the pro-ject they call the T V A.
now they are in ear-nest and Ten-nes-see's gone wild.

2. I see them boys a-comin', their tool kits on their arm;
They come from Clinch and Holston and many a fallen farm.
All up and down the valley they heard the glad alarm;
The government means business; it's workin' like a charm.

3. Oh, see the boys a-comin'; their government they trust.
Just hear their hammers singin'; they'll build that dam or bust.
I'm writin' Sal a letter; these words I'll surely say:
"The government has saved us; just name our weddin' day."

4. We'll build a little cabin, on Cove Creek near her home.
We'll settle down forever and never care to roam.
For things are surely movin', down there in Tennessee:
Good times for all the valley, for Sally and for me.

Darlin' Corrie

Traditional

4. The last time I seen darlin' Corrie,
   Her pistols was in her hand;
   She done kilt that revenue officer, officer,
   What took away her corn-likker man.

5. Dig me a hole in the cornfield,
   Dig me a hole in the ground;
   Oh, dig me a hole in the cornfield
   Just to lay my darlin' Corrie down.

[173]

I Am a Union Woman

Aunt Molly Jackson

1. I am a union wom-an, Just as brave as I can be,
   raised in old Ken-tuck-y, In Ken-tuck-y borned and bred,
   is the worst time on earth That __ I have ev-er saw,

I do not like the boss-es, __ And the boss-es don't like me.
And when I joined the un-ion, __ They __ called me a Roo-shian Red.
To get killed out by gun-thugs __ And __ framed up by the law.

REFRAIN

Join the C I O. O, Come join the C I O.

2. I was
3. This

4. When my husband asked the boss for a job,
   This is the words he said,
   "Bill Jackson, I can't work you, sir,
   Your wife's a Rooshian Red." [*Refrain*]

5. If you want to join a union,
   As strong as one can be,
   Join the dear old CIO,
   And come along with me. [*Refrain*]

6. We are many thousand strong,
   And I am glad to say,
   We are getting stronger
   And stronger every day. [*Refrain*]

7. The bosses ride big fine horses,
   While we walk in the mud,
   Their banner is the dollar sign,
   And ours is striped with blood. [*Refrain*]

Joe Hill

Words by *Alfred Hayes*
Music by *Earl Robinson*

3. "The copper bosses killed you, Joe;
   They shot you, Joe," says I.
   "Takes more than guns to kill a man,"
   Says Joe, "I didn't die,"
   Says Joe, "I didn't die."

4. And standing there as big as life
   And smiling with his eyes,
   Joe says, "What they forgot to kill
   Went on to organize,
   Went on to organize."

Git Back Blues
(Black, Brown, and White Blues)

William ("Big Bill") Broonzy

3. Me and a man's working side by side;
This is what it meant:
He was getting a dollar an hour,
When I was making fifty cents. [Chorus]

4. I helped to build this country,
I fought for it, too.
Now I guess that you can see
What a black man have to do. [Chorus]

(1945-1970s)

8

ATOMIC AGE TO SPACE AGE
(1945-1970s)

In a blinding flash the war was over, the atomic age begun, the United States now world leader. American folk song, once a rural staple, went urban, nourishing a whole generation that sang and responded to the crush of events in the truest broadside tradition. By the end of the forties visible cracks of fragmentation had unsettled the war-united society. A war of nerves pressing heavily on the pedal of fear forced the realization that winning the war didn't mean winning the peace: HUAC, the Smith Act, Taft-Hartley; strikes, lockouts, trials; oaths (treason and loyalty), air lifts, exodus—city to suburb. The fifties survived cold war, Korean War, fallout; H-bomb, sputnik, Little Rock; beats, jets; flying saucers, computerized conformity. Clash and conscience shook up the sixties with Bay of Pigs, space shots, assassinations; freedom rides, Watts, civil rights; criminal rights, political trials, Vietnam; moon, earth, crescendo for peace. Noisy times, angry times; in the air, love, hate, fire, and pot; in the streets, middle-aged with teen-aged turning the country around. In the seventies the country endured Kent State, Wounded Knee, Watergate; stagflation, energy crisis, crisis upon crisis; a brutally disenchanted citizenry stoned into apathy and despair. Too much turmoil, too little tranquility, unleashed a torrent of songs: "Talking Atomic Blues," "What Have They Done to the Rain?," "Little Boxes," "Blowin' in the Wind"; "I Ain't Marchin' Any More," "The Cities Are Burning," "Garbage!," "Automation," "Too Old to Work," "Spacey Jones," "Now That the Buffalo's Gone," "This Old World Is Changing Hands."

World War II victory revels telecast from streets to living rooms to bars escalated joy in 1945. Bess Meyerson (first Jewish Miss America) was crowned in Atlantic City, New York State's Anti-Discrimination Commission set up, subtle discrimination exposed in *Gentlemen's Agreement*. The color curtain pierced; by Jackie Robinson in sports; by Edith Mae Irby in a southern medical school. Blacks stuck in cities, whites freely settled suburbs; unions turned right, leaving folk music behind. Giant corporations fractured families and friendships. Social problems produced *The Lost Weekend, The Snake Pit,* Arthur Miller and Tennessee Williams plays; books by Bellow, Capote, Mailer; modern dance by high priestess Martha Graham; nonobjective art by abstract expressionists. Silly Putty, Kinsey's sex report, canasta dominated fads. The New Look in fashion, full, midcalf skirts; the new look in housing, quonset hut, trailer home, prefab, ranch house, split level—levels below Bucky Fuller's visions. Shaping split-level interiors and lives were designers Charles Eames, Raymond Loewy, Herman Miller, Russel Wright; plastic dishes to glass curtains and coffee tables; shag rugs, sling chairs, womb chairs (cosy if mother worked). The new baby sitter, a million TV sets. Millions sold on Spock's baby bible, diaper service, electric blankets, aluminum foil, college degrees. Colleges accepted married students; student fathers combined homework, housework, baby care. The promise of the future brightened with Fulbrights, the Marshall Plan, the U.N.; speeded up with jets, instant Polaroid, instant Xerox; amplified with LP, hi-fi, deafening guitar. Life's accelerated pace welcomed Dramamine, antihistamine, penicillin, cortisone; group health, B_{12}, frozen orange juice.

Cold war politics split headlines with splitting Democrats (Progressives and Dixiecrats), Truman the victor. Eden Ahbez anticipated the hippie with "Nature Boy," crooned by Nat King Cole; Charles Winick, unisex with "The New People"; dancer Pearl Primus, black consciousness. Equally prophetic: Alwin Nikolais's total dance theater telegraphed alienation; Jackson Pollock's spattered canvases, James Jones's obscenities (*From Here to Eternity*). The 38th Parallel a place to watch on the map.

TV shows most watched in the early days: Milton Berle, Jackie Gleason, "Show of Shows," "Studio One"; Howdy Doody, Superman, Lucy, and Danny Thomas; Ed Sullivan (on twenty-three years), Liberace, Perry Como, "Your Hit Parade." Perpetual hit, "What's My Line?"; Frank Costello's line questionable, his hands starred on Kefauver hearings, cops on "Dragnet." Sex kitten MM shot to stardom in *The Asphalt Jungle*, as films matured with *High Noon* and grew gimicky with Cinerama and 3-D.

The mature male—gray flannel suit, button-down collar (buttoned-down mind), black-tie, horn-rimmed glasses, attaché case—turned organization man, commuter, part-time father, do it-yourselfer, power-tool maven. Miracle fibers made fabrics stretchable, bondable, carefree; drip-dry, permanent-press whisked through detergents. Carefree too, women's fake furs in winter, bikinis in summer, slacks year round. *Femme fatale*-ity—choker, cincher, crinoline—briefly revived. Mother-daughter fashions released with Barbie dolls, *Guys and Dolls*, "Today," "Tonight," color TV, TV dinners; defense drills, H-bombs, fallout on minds.

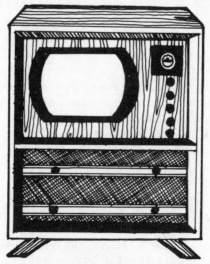

Eisenhower cut police action in Korea, air-raid drills at home. Campus panty raids, *Catcher in the Rye*, Johnny Ray's "Cry" a far cry from Ginsberg's "Howl," Krassner's (underground) *Realist*. Tripping *On the Road* with Kerouac, footloose, living loose—ahead in time. A heady brew—Zen, bop, pot—as foreign to the silent generation as Hiss and the Hollywood Ten. McCarthyism—denounced by Murrow on the tube, I.F. Stone in print—blacklists, witch hunts, hearings accused many, jailed some, exiled more, electrocuted two, the Rosenbergs. The Supreme Court decision banning school segregation shocked the nation; Autherine Lucy, the University of Alabama. Rosa Parks ticked off the Montgomery bus boycott, refus-

ing to sit in the back; interstate transit integrated soon after. As segregation barriers slowly dropped, communication barriers rapidly rose: "Yakety Yak," Gerald McBoing-Boing, *Rebel Without a Cause*. The bond and breakwater, money, cut off feelings as Americans went deep into a buying binge, sales and sound volume up. Hidden persuaders sold appliances, gadgets, packaging, "togetherness"—the family that prayed together stayed together. These were the green years, selling chlorophyll toothpaste, deodorant, dog food; the Arrid years, selling social acceptance, sex, and instant success. The instant success of Scrabble, Hula Hoops, coon-skin caps, limited and short-lived next to costly status symbols: boat, beach house, conspicuous car, muted mink; engineered kitchen, conversation pit, pedestal chair. With expense accounts and credit cards, old-fashioned thrift went the way of Fly-Now-Pay-Later; gone too, the penny postcard. Aerospace and electronics took off, agri-

business bloomed, big business fostered industrial sprawl: parks, shopping centers, service industries, rent-a-this, rent-a-that, drive-in banks, burger stands.

Ford Foundation grants to education, $500 million; comic book sales, 100 million; teen-age market, billions—fashions, fads, and 45's spinning no-message rock in an era of brinksmanship, rackeetering *On the Waterfront*. The spread of rackets, crime, terror tactics, and juvenile delinquency deepened, decentralized: larceny and vandalism in suburbs, zip guns and switch blades in cities. Smoking, drinking, and pill-popping (young and old) swamped therapist's office and emergency room; tranquilized mental patients meanwhile released. The Salk vaccine tamed polio; *Arthritis and Common Sense* prescribed nature's way; health foods and megavitamins the future wave.

The Road to Miltown and *Peyton Place* found Americans upset by *The Man with the Golden Arm*; the Becks's *Connection*; Dada's child, the happening. Less upsetting, more traditional: film epics *Ben Hur*, *The Ten Commandments*, classic books, classic theater, on Broadway, off-Broadway, community theater, Percy Faith, Lawrence Welk. If Wright's Guggenheim, Calder's mobiles, and UFO's intrigued, sputnik triggered sheer panic. The push-pull response: all-out teamwork; more math and science in the classroom, a clarion call for teachers, engineers, scientists (in surplus supply by the seventies).

The hardly comatose fifties closed with a crack in the picture window, urban renewal (really removal), fifty states (Alaska and Hawaii newly added), a warning from Ike to watch the military-industrial complex. Life's problems amplified: goods not God; things not people; hearts empty, pockets full; an affluent society spiritually and morally bankrupt.

A sunburst exploding through the cloud cover of the previous decade revealed Kennedy's New Frontier, reviving hope, Rooseveltian faith in the future. Live press conferences on TV, Peace Corps, witty Stevenson at the U.N., Telstar, a man on the moon. If Jack had charisma, Jackie had class. Summoned by Camelot's handsome, youthful, vigorous king, artists, intellectuals, blacks swept into Washington on a new tide of patriotism: "Ask not what your country can do for you—ask what you can do for your country." Loyal subjects flooded the capital. Queen of the Beautiful People, bouffant hairdo to pared-down elegance, Jackie brought glamor and culture to the White House—Caroline, John-John, Kennedy clan and Compound exemplifying family togetherness, top-drawer competitiveness. Compared to the Kennedys, the Dulleses (John Foster and Allen) seemed Neanderthal. With Bobby's shirt-sleeved diplomacy at home (integration), Jack's stylish diplomacy abroad, democracy was arrogantly sold inside/outside U.S. borders; hard-sell/soft-sell bordering on disaster for the nuclear family.

Everything seemed A-OK. Then came the Bay of Pigs, Laos, Vietnam; the Berlin Wall, Khrushchev wall, Cuban crisis. Sit-ins, march-ins, pray-ins, Martin Luther King's nonviolence violated by freedom riders, Ku Klux riders, sheriffs, soldiers, tear gas, hoses till that gorgeous August day when two hundred thousand peacefully marched on Washington. The day things went beserk in Dallas everything blew apart— people and country—Kennedy the great and great expectations killed in motion. Instant replay replayed to death, his assassin assassinated on fifty million home TV screens. Then, Air Force One, a riderless horse, a son's salute, images blurred by the tears of a nation.

Lyndon Johnson's Great Society realized the New Frontier by strongarming Congress: War on Poverty, Civil Rights Bill, Medicare, Medicaid, Social Security raised. Lady Bird, Lynda Bird, Lucie Bird beautified America as it came apart at the seams; generation gap, credibility gap, integration gap. CORE, SNCC, Muslims, Malcolm X, Black Panthers, black power inflamed, inner cities aflame. Steaming soul, mindless rock, mindless pop; Mouseketeer, missile, "Mission Impossible," Vietnam, followed "Batman" and "Star Trek" into the living room.

The unreality of guns and butter, the reality of draft notices, death notices, put the peace movement on its feet: vigiling, fasting, leafleting; demonstrating, draft-card burning, counseling; GI coffee houses, civil disobedience. Paddy wagons, jails, trials; peace symbols, V-signs, inverted flags. Flag-waving ("My country—love it or leave it"), decals, lapel pins, bumper stickers; Middle America vs. counterculture, hardhat vs. longhaired youth.

Search and destroy missions in Vietnam, search and discover missions in space. The regularity of splashdowns, black boxes, basket cases slowly penetrating American consciousness brutalized by King and Kennedy murders, inner-city riots, urban guerrilla warfare, police brutality, Weathermen blasts. With violence stepped up, LBJ stepped down, Armstrong stepped on the moon. On earth, ecology; on campus, Kent State, a coda to a violent decade.

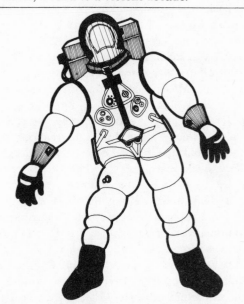

Suddenly everything changed. Counterculture counterconformity. "All in the Family," "American Family," parents without partners, *Portnoy's Complaint*. Establishment. Hippie, yippie, house wrecking. Found art, "do your thing." Stop at two. Communal living, group isolation. Earthworks. Commune hog-farm drop-city crash-pad. Speed. "Unsafe at any speed." Drag racing, pooper scoopers, Pampers. Pollution. Pothead, acidhead, waterbed. Queensize, kingsize peep show. Porno, *Penthouse, Viva, Cosmo* "letting it all hang out." Topless go-go girl or guy. Straight, gay, any way: homo- hetero- a-sexual. Transsexual, unisexual. Women's lib, men's lib, Masters-Johnson, *Ms.* Title VII, "Seize the Time." "Say it out loud, I'm black and I'm proud." Afro, corn row, hair pick, Water Pik.

Aboveground pool. Cool. Sealab, skylab, skindive, skydive. Jumpsuit. Skyjack, hijack, rip-off. Baaaad scene. Right on, graffiti, body paint, paint-by-number. New math, old math, ITA. Pass-fail, fail-safe. Security blanket, thermal blanket. Space station, Woodstock nation. Gas line, pipeline, *Shaft.* Wheat deal, oil deal, no deal. Glitch, kitsch, superschlock, *Love Story.*

Who's Afraid of Virginia Woolf? Fritz the Cat. Top dog, attack dog. Bolts, locks, *Hair.* Hair-blowing, mind-blowing. No-bra bra. Hot pants, panty hose, bulletproof clothes. Army surplus, T-shirt tux. Tote bag, buckskin, barefoot. Earthshoe, sandal. Clunky platform clumping clog. Campy, kookie, kinky, kicky. Mini, maxi, mod. Body suit, body language. Like now, like wow! Pop, Op, bubble-top.

Inflatables, deflatables: furniture, ego, house and home. Astrodome, hot foam, shaved dome. Tie-dye, My Lai, government lie. Corporate spy. Natural high. Babies, basketry, nursing, cursing. Conceptual art, minimal art. Copout. Tune out, tune in. Inner clock, culture shock, time lag, real drag. Dr. K. *Dr. Strangelove,* SST, PVC. LNG. Radiation, alienation. Containerization. Collapsable, convertible. Disposable, monument, mace. Maser, laser, microfilm, microfiche. Rerun, recall, seeking, streaking. Zap, Zen, monk, mantra. Jews for Jews. Jews for Jesus, Jesus freaks, food freaks, fashion freaks. Far out, freakout. Readout, printout, output, input. Loco, logo, underground press. Tape deck, disco-tech. LP-TV 8-track cassette.

Head set, head shop. Flower power. Brown power, red power. Kid power, "Kung Fu." Action figure GI Joe. Nerf ball, super ball. Super bowl. Gourmet feast, ghetto famine, fast-food franchise, freeze dried. Snow machine, cash machine, "all systems go." Jogging, jiving, hustling, hassling. Mass transit. Cycling, recycling. Opting, co-opting. Seed strip, nostalgia trip. Nonsked, skimobile, Miracle Mile. Dance collective, street dance, dance therapy. Clergy conflicts. Right to abort, right to adopt, right to death, right to life. Death of Life.

Living complex. Prestressed concrete. Indoor-outdoor carpeting. Cluster housing, urban co-op, homestead, A-frame, condominium. Module. Built-in, knockdown, group encounter. Pentagon Papers, primal therapy, primitive art. Heart valve, transplant, pacemaker, Pap test. Test ban, SALT talk, Telex. Tunnel diode. Solid-state, micro-mini, skirt to circuit. Closed circuit, printed circuit, pocket brain, biofeedback. Beeper. Paramedic, paraplegic. Valium, VD, IUD. Pill. Swinging, swapping, surfing singles. *Boys in the Band,* Muscle Beach, male scent, nude dude.

Classless look, instant book. Instant beauty. Liner, sealer, wiglet, fall. Curling comb, silicone. Nosecone,

erogenous zone. Princess phone. Hangup, hang in, "Laugh-In." Button, button, panic button. *Jesus Christ Superstar.* "Float like a butterfly, sting like a bee." Buzz, fuzz. Bugging, mugging. Stereo systems, security systems. Unchained chain. Schools without walls, open classrooms. Headstart, "Sesame Street." Street theater, theater absurd. Radical chic, radical right, radical left, new left tactic. Spontaneous combustion, *In the Heat of the Night, In Cold Blood.*

The flaring flames of the sixties turned to glowing embers in the seventies; the new energy source "The People, Yes"—crime in the streets, law and order notwithstanding. Truth and love, positive fallout from a fiery decade, placed integrity first, hypocrisy last. Vietnam "peace with honor" dragged Horatio Alger, *The Terminal Man,* from quagmire to Watergate. Hearings, tapes, subpoenas; judges, juries, executive privilege. The agony of Agnew's plea bargaining. From foot pedal to phone (Rosemary's stretch) an unbridgeable 18½-minute gap, silences louder than words. Nixon's right to withhold, the nation's right to know, a head-on collision: the Supreme Court curbing presidential power, placing evidence on the scales of justice. The weight of proof so damaging, the price so high, the president fled into private life.

The wheels of democracy greased by the Twenty-Fifth Amendment (presidential succession) kept the country running and put Gerald Ford in the driver's seat, Rockefeller a heartbeat away (months later). The existing economic turndown slipped into economic crisis by mid-seventies, fueled by energy crisis. The volume of depression noises rose with unemployment figures as gross national product fell. Caught off guard, many people in the world's richest country were forced to decide between heating and eating. Food stamps, garbage skimming, pet-food dinners— subsistence bill of fare for fixed income and welfare level. Stagflation: system, city, soul, suffering severe decay. Too little sensitivity, too much fear, distortion out of proportion, priorities out of order, balance wheel out of kilter. Prognosis: unknown; self-healing a vital factor. Will the country take its medicine?

Unwilling to settle for muddling through, a painful period of transition, Americans found themselves on the precipice of a new potential, faced for the first time with multiple choices, conscious choices, a quantum leap toward individual identity. With a new openness, a trust in self-renewal, people started searching for fresh solutions to nagging problems. Old age: lack and neglect, lack of respect. Tax structure: guaranteed income or negative tax? Family structure. Institutions: education to edifice, waste to work ethic. What will go? What will stay? Dependence/responsibility: Will the gap be closed? Man/machines: Will intermediate technology rehumanize? In a shrinking world, will Americans replace outmoded might and right with enlightened self-interest?

Every age has always had a few artists projecting the future. In 1945 with all hell breaking loose in outer space, musicians in every sphere, classic to jazz, country to folk, explored inner space. If the new was limited in audience appeal, the opposite was true of the public's appetite for older musical forms. The volume of music swelled to undreamed-of proportions on the air, in concert hall and classroom; the impact of LP and TV, private foundation and public endowment bringing more music into daily lives—live, canned, a mixture of both—a broader spectrum.

Classical composers with a greater variety of tools at their disposal expanded existing forms, experimented with new techniques: twelve-tone, electronic, computer, chance. Less concerned with communicating than experimenting, the majority of postwar composers tuned into the twelve-tone scale, using it in one form or another. Taking the serial concept one step further, Milton Babbitt codified it, expanding it on the one hand, exercising total control on the other, electronically fusing the roles of composer and performer. Tape recorders, electronic generators, filtering and reverberating devices, scores edited by scissors and splicing block—basic equipment, basic techniques—grew in sophistication and precision with the synthesizer. Concretely creating in his medium, the electronic composer experienced the total control of a painter or sculptor. The tinkering of others was to produce electrified rock, "Switched-On Bach."

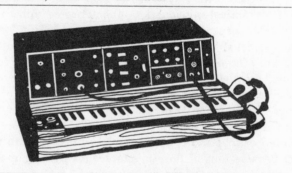

First cousin to electronic music, computer music, pioneered by Hiller and Isaacson (Iliac Suite, 1956). If composers of electronic and computer music sought control over material, an opposite impulse led creators to reduce it. Cage, Feldman, Wolf, and Brown, using chance or random methods furnished musical raw material to be ordered by performers, creating a new style of virtuosity. In lieu of raw material some scores suggested physical activity to initiate sounds;

in others, instruments altered by tinfoil, hammers (Cage's prepared piano),became an integral part of the composition.

Sound shaping time, rather than shaped by it, released new energies. By the sixties the likes of Elliot Carter, tuning fork to the ground, picked up conflicting vibrations; counterpointing time values and tempi, opened up communication between composer and listener.

The crosscurrents of old and new saw a breakthrough called the third stream, elements of jazz seeping into classics, classic elements into jazz. At the same moment in time, waves of jazz breaking on the beach rippled cool, funky, and freaky. By the late forties the heat of early after-hours jams had cooled. Principal innovators: Miles Davis and Charlie Parker. Successfully grafted to jazz: french horn, flute, tuba; musical elegance, restraint (written, unwritten), complexities, unresolved chords, deliberately misplaced beats. Bop (progressive chamber jazz), a voyage inward, moved outward as hard bop (funky jazz) in the fifties.

Gerry Mulligan, Stan Getz, Herbie Mann added a layer of complexity; John Lewis's MJQ refinement —more baroque than black. Distilling similar classical forms, white pianist Dave Brubeck & Co.; pulling the style further from its roots, the intricate inventions of Lennie Tristano and Herbie Hancock. In reaction to highly polished, inbred jazz, the harshness of hard bop, the path back to the roots led by Horace Silver, Art Blakey, Monk, and Mingus. The new breed—the cool of bop crossed with the hot of New Orleans—funky jazz.

Freaky or free-form jazz, so atonal as to be dubbed nonjazz, scrapped tune and steady beat, splintering notes into an almost spontaneous ecstasy, players virtually relying on ESP to pick up each other's ideas. Jazz messengers heralding the black militancy of the sixties, John Coltrane, Ornette Coleman, and Archie Shepp horned their way through the seething expressionism of the new thing. Along with flames of black rage, jazz died down, not rekindled till the seventies.

Through gospel singer Mahalia Jackson the black message touched white consciousness—the medium, blues. Jazz organist Ray Charles, his blues singing overlaid with gospel passion: the embodiment of rhythm and blues. A raw strain surfaced with Little Richard—frantic, falsetto-shrieking, hipflinging, piano beating—a piece of lurid showmanship. Taking the same black and white keys, Fats Domino's jackhammer approach—plodding pounding bass, roaming right hand, grating voice—added his touch to what would become rock 'n' roll.

Rock really got rolling with snarling, white, country boy Elvis Presley, gyrating his way to fame. Suggestive singing, erotic guitar handling turned on teenagers coast to coast; the winning combination—rockabilly (hillbilly)—rocked to rhythm and blues. With "Hound Dog" and "Blue Suede Shoes," rockabilly went national in the footprints of the Crewcuts' "Sh-Boom," the first rock record to rocket the pop charts. "Rock Around the Clock" rocketed Bill Haley and his

Comets to stardom, the first pop group with distinctively unraunchy rock style. Yet the same group, the same piece, the nucleus of the *Blackboard Jungle* film score, came through as rebellious music, its raucous driving beat expressing youth's anger; much the same way unpalatable material was made palatable by a wholesome Pat Boone in white bucks.

Stylistically, rock fissioned into death rock, baroque rock, raga rock, acid rock (Joplin, Hendrix, and Jefferson Airplane); in the seventies glitter rock. Rock was everywhere: portable radios, car radios; the disk jockey, king; youthful subjects tuning in day and night. Every live show sold out, drowned out by screaming, stomping, fainting fans—autograph hounds to groupies, fanatical collectors.

Dick Clark's "American Bandstand" going national in '57 kept the rock works moving for teens. And move they did: the boogaloo, the frug, funky chicken, hully-gully, jerk, mashed potato, Watusi. Most popular, the twist, the making of Chubby Checker, the dancing lounge, and discothèque.

With motorcycles roaring off in the distance, lights and psychedelic sounds fading, hard rock came back harder and heavier with Chuck Berry, the Everly and Eisley brothers, Jerry Lee Lewis, the Platters—their oldies but goodies pitched on TV. Exploiting the R & R revival, Sha Na Na came along with mock rock. In a word, the height of rock culture was Wood-

stock—amps up, violence down, stars, nonstars, audience starred—a spectacular statement of the youth cult; a world filled with music, drugs, love—most of it free.

The spectacular emergence of soul triggered by Watts sparked a rhythm and blues revival—black and white. The personification of "black is beautiful": the soul sounds of James Brown, Roberta Flack, Aretha Franklin, and Al Green; Isaac Hayes, Jackson Five, Gladys Knight and the Pips, Curtis Mayfield, Otis Redding; Smokey Robinson, Diana Ross, Supremes, Temptations, and Stevie Wonder.

If worlds apart, the so-called Detroit sound (soul) and the Nashville sound (country-western)—both based in rhythm and blues—have always shared an earthiness. The country-western touch quicker and lighter, its folksiness anchored by guitar. Country blues and ballads, old and new, now and then, music in the folk form about real folks: love, work, God and country; struggling in the real world, driving trucks, slinging hash, growing food, pumping gas. Old and new country-westerners: Chet Atkins, Glenn Campbell, Lester Flatt, Red Foley, and Merle Haggard; John Hartford, Doug Kershaw, Loretta Lynn, and Wayne Newton; Marty Robbins, Earl Scruggs, Mason Williams, Tammy Wynette. Working country-western, rock, and folk: Johnny Cash.

If country-western has sought to preserve a way of life, folk has sought to preserve the thread of life—past, present, and future. From the thirties onward it has reflected shifting population and points of view from city to country, simplicity to sophistication. The new folk, once the music of common folk, was taken over by musical missionaries—the educated minstrel, the union organizer—selling an idea, assuaging the soul. Although sung from the heart, they never really captured the heart of millhand, miner, or migrant, for whom they were written. Once the cause was won, polemics were forgotten along with the songs. In the move from union hall to concert hall folk was removed still one step further from its original source. Audiences that had cut their teeth on Woody Guthrie fast became fans of the Almanacs, championing their socially conscious songs, cheering their hoots. For the apolitical, the traditional recordings of Burl Ives and Josh White, the spirituals of Paul Robeson and Marian Anderson. Pete Seeger, his voice never stilled by blacklisting, was to carry on the Woody Guthrie tradition, a pivotal force for social change.

The Weavers (Seeger, Lee Hayes, Fred Hellerman, Ronnie Gilbert), the first folk group to make it outside folk circles, recorded Leadbelly's "Goodnight Irene" in 1950, up-sounding music, no message in sight. Once the Kingston Trio hit the charts with "Tom Dooley" the folk star was on the rise: Peter, Paul, and Mary; the Limelighters; duets, quartets; on the rise too, sheet music, LP, banjo, and guitar sales. School systems got in the act, children singing more and more folk material; middle-class whites, ghetto blacks mimicking their mentors. On campuses, in coffee houses, hip cafés, folk was *in*, side by side with social satire: Mort Sahl, Shelley Berman, Dick Gregory, Lenny Bruce.

Changing times saw topical material overtake traditional, lyricism once more overlaid with message. A singing youth movement intent on burying Jim Crow threw force and energy into walk-ins, sit-ins, pray-ins, picket lines, marches, freedom rides; the opposing force cattle-prodding, tear-gassing, hosing, jailing. The unifying spirit; freedom songs soaring over the barricades. "Blowin' in the Wind," Bob Dylan's personal statement, soared above traditional freedom songs and spirituals, many with updated verses. Equally fervent, the personal statements of Eric Anderson, Len Chandler, Jimmy Collier; Peter LaFarge, Phil Ochs, Tom Paxton; Malvina Reynolds, Buffy Sainte-Marie, and Nina Simone. Important interpreters (sometime-composers): Joan Baez, Judy Collins, Barbara Dane, Odetta. Freedom singers invaded the South, songbags full of music most blacks had learned to be ashamed of. Singing the songs of Leadbelly and Big Bill Broonzy, they gave back a gift of dignity and stature. Disillusioned, the movement shifted from nonviolence to violence, patience to black power, folk singing to karate.

Yoga, flowers, beads and incense, flowing hair and free-form life-styles permeated the peace movement in the same space and time. The cementing agent: freedom songs, peace songs, new ones, old ones, sung by a white middle class that took to the streets. All ages, all persuasions: parents with children in back-

packs, strollers, wagons; aged and infirm with canes, crutches, wheelchairs; conservatives shoulder to shoulder with radicals. As the movement gained momentum, disruptive elements shocked and rocked; bombs, not ballads, filled the air.

Dylan, the seer of the singing movement,* rocked folkniks when he went electric at Newport; the boos soon drowned out by the Byrds's folk-rock version of "Mr. Tambourine Man," brilliantly plugging into a drug-heavy rock culture. Buffy Sainte-Marie turned up the volume with "Cod'ine," the Jefferson Airplane with "White Rabbit." Adding to the decibel din, folk-rockers Sonny and Cher, Gary McGuire, Country Joe and the Fish; distilling it for the masses, the Lovin' Spoonful, the Mamas and the Papas; softening the sound, Simon and Garfunkel, their soft, cerebral, gentle rock reopening ears to the earthy blues of Lightnin' Hopkins, B.B. King, Muddy Waters, and Richie Havens's progressive-folk.

As folk-rock increasingly smacked of life-style, not music style, sound and subject ran second to personal image. Heading for interesting planes on the heels of Crosby, Stills, Nash, and Young were pop-folk communicators Harry Chapin, John Denver, Waylon Jennings, and Carole King; Kris Kristofferson, Seals and Crofts, Carly Simon, and James Taylor. With them a new individualism surfaced—style, statement, person so completely fused—private thoughts went public. Even Dylan, the beacon of a whole generation, had internalized the light, exposing a searing inner landscape.

How very American that individualism was redefined as the curve of the new revolution gently propelled the nation into reexamining, reevaluating every concept, every institution—democracy to family. Perpetual motion, so crucial to a country that has never settled down, never stopped rocking, has always been the wellspring of its unique vitality. The strongly individual character of this vitality, ever a dominant key of American folk song, is now headed for even more glorious resolutions in the new music as more and more people tune in to the sounds of the universe.

* Unfortunately, permission for Bob Dylan songs could not be obtained.

Last Night I Had the Strangest Dream

Ed McCurdy

1. 3. Last night I had the strang - est dream, I'd
2. And when the pa - per was all signed, and a

ev - er had be - fore. I They
mil - lion cop - ies made,

dreamed the world had all a - greed to
all joined hands and all bowed their heads to and

put an end to war. I
grate - ful prayers were prayed. And the

dreamed   I   saw   a   might - y   room,   the
peo - ple   in   the   streets   be - low   the were

room   was   full   of   men,   And the
danc - ing round and round,   While

pa - per   they   were   sign - ing   said   they'd
swords and   guns   and   u - ni - forms   were

nev - er   fight   a - gain.
scat - tered   on   the   ground.   *D.C. al Fine*

Tom Dooley

Collected, adapted, and arranged by
Frank Warner, John A. Lomax, and Alan Lomax

Little Boxes

Malvina Reynolds

Sprightly

1. Lit-tle box-es on the hill-side, Lit-tle box-es made of tick-y tack-y, Lit-tle
3. And the peo-ple in the hous-es All ___ went to the u-ni-ver-si-ty, ___ Where they

box-es on the hill-side, Lit-tle box-es all the same. 2. There's a
all were put in box-es And they came out all the same. 4. And there's

green one and a pink one And a blue one and a yel-low one, And they're
doc-tors and there's law-yers, And bus-'ness ex - ec-u-tives, And they're

all made out of tick-y tack-y And they all look just the same.
all made out of tick-y tack-y And they all look just the same.

cross over R.H.

5. And they all play on the golf course
   And drink their martinis dry,
   And they all have pretty children
   And the children go to school.

6. And the children go to summer camp
   And then to the university,
   Where they are put in boxes
   And they come out all the same.

7. And the boys go into business
   And marry and raise a family
   In boxes made of ticky tacky
   And they all look just the same.

Automation

Joe Glazer

see:
me.
Pete!"   And a

No - thing but but - tons and
There ___ was a ro - bot sit - ting
great   big me - chan - i - cal

bells and lights ___ All o - ver the fac - to - ry.
in   the seat ___ Where the fore - man used to be. ___
voice boomed out: ___ "All your bud - dies are ob - so - lete." ___

4. I was scared, scared, scared, I was worried, I was sick
   As I left the factory.
   I decided that I had to see the president
   Of the whole darn company.
   When I got up to his office, he was rushing out the door
   With a scowl upon his face,
   'Cause there was a great big mechanical executive
   Sitting in the president's place.

5. I went home, home, home to my ever-loving wife
   And told her 'bout the factory.
   She hugged me and she kissed me and she cried a little bit
   As she sat on my knee.
   I don't understand all the buttons and the lights
   But one thing I will say,
   "I thank the Lord that love's still made
   In the good old-fashioned way."

The Ballad of Ira Hayes

Peter LaFarge

Freely

I - ra Hayes, _____ I - ra Hayes.

CHORUS   Moderately

Call him drunk - en I - ra Hayes, He won't
drunk - en I - ra Hayes, But his

an - swer an - y more; Not the whis - key drink - in'
land is still as dry, And his ghost is ly - ing

In - dian, Not the ma - rine that went to war.
thirst - y In the ditch where I - ra died.

Fine

RECITATION

1. Ga - ther 'round me peo - ple, there's a sto - ry I would
land of the Pi - ma In - di - ans, a proud and no - ble

tell A - bout a brave young In - di - an you
band, Who farmed the Phoe - nix val - ley in

should re - mem - ber well; From the
A - ri - zo - na land. Call him

2. Down their ditches for a thousand years, the waters grew Ira's people's crops,
   Till the white man stole their water rights and their sparklin' water stopped.
   Now Ira's folks were hungry and their farm grew rocks and weeds,
   When war came Ira volunteered and forgot the white man's greed. [*Chorus*]

3. They battled up Iwo Jima hill, two hundred and fifty men,
   But only twenty-seven lived to walk back down again;
   And when the fight was over and Old Glory raised,
   Among the men who held it high was the Indian, Ira Hayes. [*Chorus*]

4. Ira Hayes returned a hero, celebrated through the land,
   He was wined and speeched and honored, everybody shook his hand;
   But he was just a Pima Indian—no money, no crops, no chance;
   At home nobody cared what Ira done, and when do the Indians dance? [*Chorus*]

5. Then Ira started drinking hard, jail often was his home,
   They let him raise the flag and lower it as you'd throw a dog a bone.
   He died drunk early one morning, alone in the land he'd fought to save,
   Two inches of water in a lonely ditch was the grave of Ira Hayes. Yes, [*Chorus*]

[193]

If I Had a Hammer

(The Hammer Song)

Words by *Lee Hayes*
Music by *Pete Seeger*

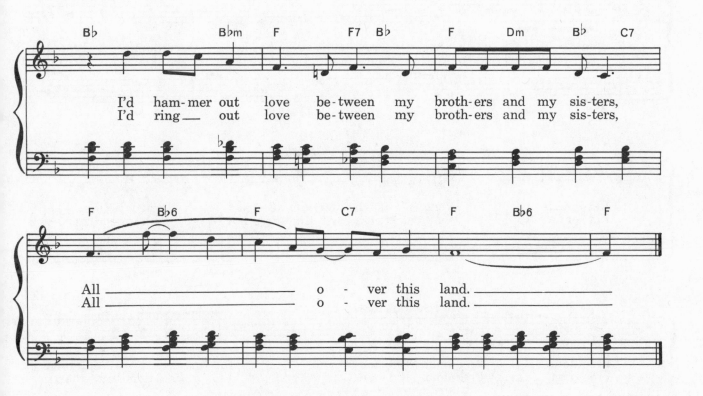

3. If I had a song, I'd sing it in the morning,
   I'd sing it in the evening, all over this land;
   I'd sing out danger, I'd sing out a warning,
   I'd sing out love between my brothers and my sisters,
      All over this land.

4. Well, I got a hammer, and I've got a bell,
   And I've got a song, all over this land;
   It's the hammer of justice, it's the bell of freedom,
   It's the song about love between my brothers and my sisters,
      All over this land.

Freedom Rider

Words by *Marilyn Eisenberg*
Traditional Music

3. They took me up to jail in a big black paddy wagon—
   Freedom, Freedom Rider.
   I sang all the way, my spirit wasn't dragging—
   Freedom, Freedom Rider.
   We shall overcome and we shall not be moved,
   And climbing Jacob's ladder too.

4. Well, I went before the judge and what did he say—
   Freedom, Freedom Rider.
   "You've breached the peace, now in jail you must stay,"
   Freedom, Freedom Rider.
   "Pay two hundred dollars because you are so guilty;
   Stay in jail for four months too."

5. I didn't pay my fine, although I want to be free—
   Freedom, Freedom Rider.
   They carried me off to the penitentiary—
   Freedom, Freedom Rider.
   "I'll throw you in the hole, I'll take away your mattress,
   You damn Yankee agitator, you!"

6. Now behind the bars I keep singing this song—
   Freedom, Freedom Rider.
   Freedom's comin', and it won't be long—
   Freedom, Freedom Rider.
   I'm a Freedom Rider, he's a Freedom Rider,
   You can be a Freedom Rider too.

[196]

Old Man Atom
(A Talking Atomic Blues)

Text by *Vern Partlow*
Music by *Irving Bito*

Lyrics beneath the staves:

ma, Na - ga - sa - ki, _____ A - la - mo - gor - do, _____

____ Bi - ki - ni. _____ R.H. 2. The ki - ni _____

decresc. molto *pp* Boom! *ff*

3. But the atom's international, in spite of hysteria.
   It flourishes in Utah as well as Siberia,
   And whether you're black, white, red, or brown,
   The question is this, when you boil it down,
       To be or not to be,
       That is the question.

4. The answer to it all ain't military datum,
   Like who gets there fustest with the mostest atoms,
   No, the people of the world must decide their fate,
   They gotta get together, or disintegrate.
       We hold this truth to be self-evident—
       That all men may be cremated equal. [*Chorus*]

5. Yes, it's up to the people, 'cause the atom don't care.
   You can't fence him in, he's just like air.
   He doesn't give a hoot about any politics,
   Or who got what into whichever fix.
       All he wants to do is sit around
       And have his nucleus bombarded by neutrons.

6. Now the moral is this, just as plain as day,
   That Old Man Atom is here to stay.
   He's gonna stick around, that's plain to see,
   But, ah, my dearly beloved—are we?
       So, listen, folks. Here is my thesis,
       "Peace in the World" or the world in pieces. [*Chorus*]

What Have They Done to the Rain?

Society's Child

Janis Ian

The Cities Are Burning

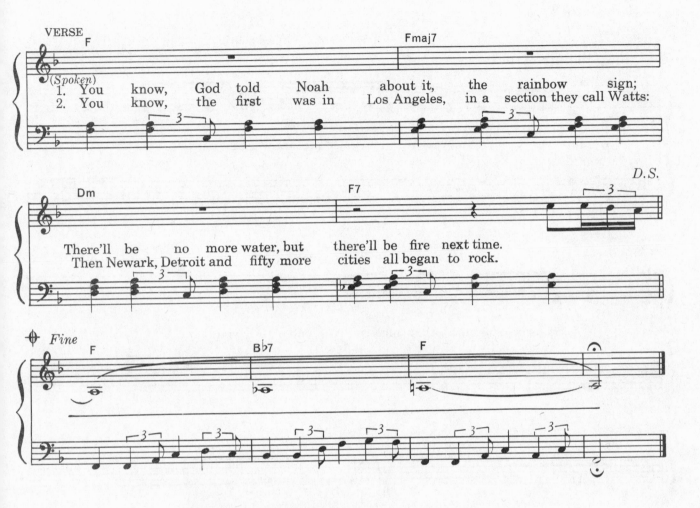

Chorus 1. The Bible's fulfillin' now
All over the U.S.A. . . . .

Chorus 2. I say these cities are burning
All over the U.S.A. . . . .

3. You know—our Father which art in heaven—
Mister Charley owed me a hundred dollars
And he didn't give me but seven—
Hallowed be thy name now—Kingdom Come—
Hadn't taken that seven, you know,
I wouldn't have got none.

Chorus 3. That's why these cities are burning
All over the U.S.A.
You know the only solution I see to this thing
Is nonviolence through Martin Luther King.

Fire and Rain

James Taylor

Now That the Buffalo's Gone

1. 2. 3. 4.

feel   in   your   heart   for   these   ones. _____

feel   you're   a   part   of   these   ones. _____   2. Oh, it's

5.

Now   that the buf - fa - lo's   gone! _____

3. When a war between nations is lost,
   The loser we know pays the cost,
   But even when Germany fell to your hands,
   Consider, dear lady, consider, dear man,
   You left them their pride and you left them their land,
   And what have you done to these ones?

4. Has a change come about Uncle Sam,
   Or are you still taking our lands?
   A treaty forever George Washington signed,
   He did, dear lady, he did, dear man,
   And the treaty's being broken by Kinzua Dam,
   And what will you do for these ones?

5. Oh, it's all in the past, you can say,
   But it's still going on here today.
   The government, now, wants the Iroquois land,
   That of the Seneca and the Cheyenne.
   It's here and it's now you must help us, dear man,
   Now that the buffalo's gone.

I Ain't Marchin' Any More

Phil Ochs

With spirit

1. Oh, I marched to the Bat - tle of New Or - leans, At the
killed my share of In - juns in a thou-sand dif-ferent fights, I was

end of the ear - ly Bri - tish war, _____ I heard
there at the Lit - tle Big Horn, _____

young land start - ed grow - in', the young blood start-ed flow - in', But
man - y men a - ly - in', I saw man - y more a - dy - in', And

I ain't march - in' an - y more. _____ 2. For I
I ain't march - in' an - y more.

INTERLUDE

It's al-ways the old to lead us to the war, Al-ways the young to fall, _____ Now, look at all we won with a sa-ber and a gun. Tell me, was it worth it all? _____

D.S. al fine

3. For I stole California from the Mexican land,
   Fought in the bloody Civil War,
   Yes, I even killed my brothers, and so many others,
   But I ain't marchin' any more.

4. For I marched to the battles of the German trench
   In a war that was bound to end all wars;
   I must have killed a million men, and now they want me back again,
   But I ain't marchin' any more. [*Interlude*]

5. For I flew the final mission in the Japanese skies,
   Set off the mighty mushroom roar,
   When I saw the cities burnin', I knew that I was learnin'
   That I ain't marchin' any more.

6. Now the labor leader's screamin' when they close the missile plants,
   United Fruit screams at the Cuban shore,
   Call it "Peace" or call it "Treason," call it "Love" or call it "Reason,"
   But I ain't marchin' any more.

Where Have All the Flowers Gone?

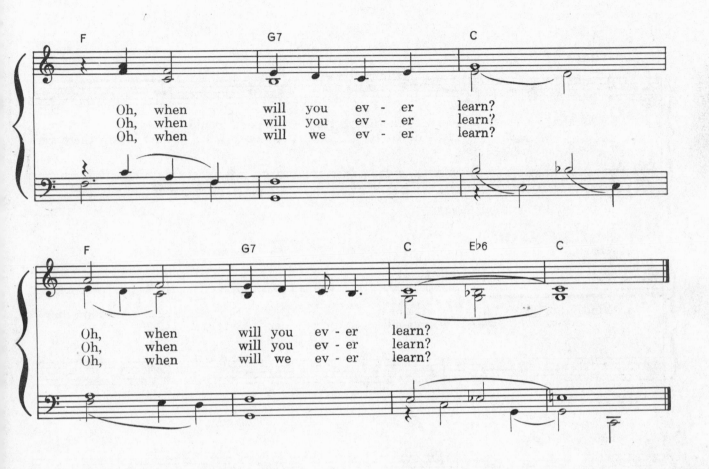

4. Where have all the soldiers gone?
   Long time passing.
Where have all the soldiers gone?
   Long time gone.
Where have all the soldiers gone?
They've gone to graveyards, ev'ry one.
Oh, when will they ever learn?
Oh, when will they ever learn?

5. Where have all the graveyards gone?
   Long time passing.
Where have all the graveyards gone?
   Long time ago.
Where have all the graveyards gone?
   They're covered with flowers, ev'ry one.
Oh, when will they ever learn?
Oh, when will they ever learn?

6. [*Repeat verse 1.*]

Pinkville Helicopter

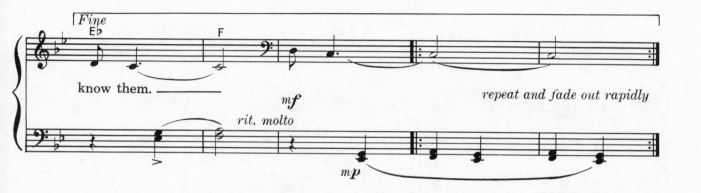

know them. _____

mf

rit. molto

repeat and fade out rapidly

mp

3. They were on their way out when below them
   They saw a little two-year-old baby,
   So they went down again and the pilot got out,
   Muttering that the world had gone crazy.

4. The baby was cradled in the pilot's arms,
   Wounded and crying and bloody,
   When a lieutenant came up and said, "Put the kid down,
   And get your chopper on out of here, buddy."

5. The pilot looked down at the lieutenant's gun
   That was smoky and hot from the killing,
   And he said, "If I have to give my life for the child,
   Then, by God, you know that I'm willing."

6. Then the gunner who stood in the helicopter's door
   Called out to the lieutenant,
   "We're calling your bluff, there's been killing enough,
   If your gun starts more, mine will end it."

7. So they flew the kids out to the medics who said,
   "War is hell, even babies get wounded."
   The pilot just looked at his gunner and shook,
   Said, "To kill them was what was intended;

8. "The things that we've seen up in Pinkville today,
   Well, we won't even try to describe them,
   But this wasn't war, it was a pack of mad dogs
   Just killing to see people dying."

9. [*Repeat verse 1.*]

We Shall Overcome

New Words and Music Adaptation by
Zilphia Horton, Frank Hamilton, Guy Carawan, and *Pete Seeger*

1. We shall o-ver-come, We shall o-ver-come,
2. We'll walk hand in hand, We'll walk hand in hand,

We shall o-ver-come some-day.
We'll walk hand in hand some-day.

Oh,

deep in my heart I do be-lieve

We shall o-ver-come some-day.

3. We are not afraid . . . today. [*Chorus*]

4. We shall stand together . . . now. [*Chorus*]

5. The truth will make us free . . . some day. [*Chorus*]

6. The Lord will see us through . . . some day. [*Chorus*]

7. We shall live in peace . . . some day. [*Chorus*]

8. We shall end Jim Crow . . . some day. [*Chorus*]

Garbage!

Bill Steele

Allegretto

grounds and sar - dine tins, Till the truck comes by on Fri - day and
hangs for thir - ty days, While the sun looks down up - on it with its

carts it all a - way, And a thou-sand trucks just like it are con -
ul - tra - vio - let tongues Till it turns to smog and set - tles down and

verg - ing on the Bay. Gar - bage, gar - bage, gar - bage,
ends up in our lungs. Gar - bage, gar - bage, gar - bage,

f

gar - bage, gar - bage, gar - bage; We're fill - ing up the sea with
gar - bage, gar - bage, gar - bage; We're fill - ing up the air with

gar-bage, gar-bage, gar-bage;   Gar-bage, gar-bage, gar-bage;   What will we do when there's
gar-bage, gar-bage, gar-bage;   Gar-bage, gar-bage, gar-bage;   What will we do when there's

no place left to put all the gar-bage?_____
no-thing left to breathe but gar-bage?_____

3. Getting home and taking off his shoes he settles down with evening news
   While the kids do homework with the TV in one ear;
   While Superman for thousandth time sells sexy dolls and conquers crime
   They dutifully learn the date-of-birth of Paul Revere.
   In the paper there's a piece about the mayor's middle name,
   And he gets it done in time to watch the all-star Bingo game.

   Garbage, garbage, garbage; garbage, garbage, garbage;
   We're filling up our minds with garbage, garbage, garbage;
   Garbage, garbage, garbage;
   What will we do when there's nothing left to hear
   And there's nothing left to read
   And there's nothing left to wear
   And there's nothing left to need
   And there's nothing left to talk about
   And there's nothing left to walk upon
   And there's nothing left to care about
   And there's nothing left to do
   And there's nothing left to see
   And there's nothing left to be but garbage?

My Ramblin' Boy

Tom Paxton

you, my ram - blin' boy. May all your

ram - blin' bring you joy. And here's to

you, my ram - blin' boy. May all your

1. 2. 3.

ram - blin' bring you joy. 2. In Tul - sa joy. *molto rit.* *pp*

R.H.

Fine

3. Late one night in a jungle camp,
   The weather it was cold and damp;
   He got the chills and he got 'em bad.
   They took the only friend I had. [*Chorus*]

4. He left me there to ramble on.
   My ramblin' pal is dead and gone.
   If when we die we go somewhere;
   I'll bet you a dollar he's ramblin' there. [*Chorus*]

Spacey Jones

Words by *Don Jacobs*
Music by *Eddie Newton*

1. Come all ye space-men if you want to hear The
o - pen up the feed - ers and don't spare the fuel,
looked at his watch and his watch was slow. He

sto - ry of a great plan - e - teer. Spac - ey
Prime up the pump so the rock - ets will cool. Gon-na rev up the
looked at the cool - ing pumps, the wa - ter was low. He looked out the

Jones was the pi - lot's name, On a fuel - burn-ing
throt - tle till I melt our tail, 'Cause I'm three days
win - dow and he saw Mars a - head, Said, "We'll make it on

4. Spacey looked down at the Martian hills,
   The rockets were screaming with an awful shrill.
   The people down below heard the rockets' moans,
   And they knew that the pilot was Spacey Jones. [*Chorus*]

5. He was sixty miles up and a-coming down fast,
   Spacey knew that the ship would never last.
   The rocket was burning and the tail was gone,
   But the turbines kept a-churning and the mail went on. [*Chorus*]

6. Now he had no wings and the tail was gone,
   The ship was overloaded 'cause the pumps weren't on.
   Spacey wrote a letter saying he done his best;
   And he put it with the mail in a big iron chest. [*Chorus*]

7. In the middle of the runway there's a great big pit,
   Which marks the spot where Spacey hit.
   When they dug up the strongbox, Spacey's note they did find,
   Saying, "I'm sorry 'bout the ship, but the mail's on time." [*Chorus*]

Kisses Sweeter Than Wine

Words by *Paul Campbell*
Music by *Joel Newman*

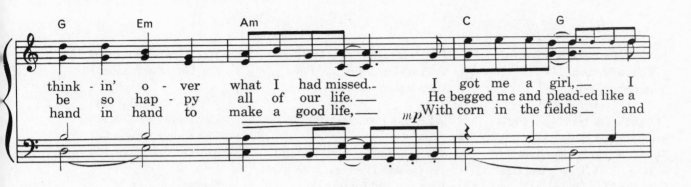

think - in' o - ver what I had missed.. I got me a girl,___ I
be so hap - py all of our life.___ He begged me and plead-ed like a
hand in hand to make a good life,___ *mp* With corn in the fields___ and

D.C.

kissed her and then___ Oh, Lord, I kissed her a - gain.___
na - tur - al man___ and then, *mf* Oh, Lord, I gave him my hand.___
wheat in the bins,___ and then, Oh, Lord, I was the fa -ther of twins.

4. Our children numbered just about four
And they all had sweethearts knock on the door.
They all got married and they didn't wait,
I was—Oh, Lord, the grandfather of eight. [*Refrain*]

5. Now we are old and ready to go.
We get to thinkin' what happened a long time ago.
We had lots of kids and trouble and pain,
But—Oh, Lord, we'd do it again. [*Refrain*]

Index of Song Titles

List of Line Drawings